THE WORLD OF
SHABBY CHIC

RACHEL ASHWELL

THE WORLD OF
SHABBY CHIC

BEAUTIFUL HOMES, MY STORY & VISION

Rizzoli
NEW YORK

New York Paris London Milan

CONTENTS

*A quiet, uncluttered loveseat—the pretty pale
slipcover detailed with a double ruffle skirt.*

1

the shabby chic story

It's been quite the journey, for Shabby Chic and for me—a journey of beauty, creativity, challenges, passion, and love. From the beginning, Shabby Chic was both my creative expression and the birth of a business. Over the years it became a dear friend and part of my identity. It brings me joy and pride that the world of Shabby Chic has touched, influenced, and inspired so many, and in doing so it has refueled my creative engine. Between us we have created a true design movement, a business and a lifestyle that is loved by us all.

an english childhood

I have lived most of my adult life in the sunny bright light of California, but, in truth, it's the rainswept windy mornings of London that really resonate with me, and to this day my inner wiring works best on a gray day with rain tapping against the window. My childhood memories are of gloomy early mornings, bundled up against the weather, scouting around flea and antique markets with my parents, flashlights ready, on the hunt for treasures and always rewarded at the end with a hot chocolate.

Dad was a secondhand book dealer; Mum, an antique-doll dealer. Dad was very well read, with a great appreciation not just for the content, but for the history and soul of books: he valued first editions, handwritten dedications and signatures, and he loved illustrated books with fine etchings. Some rooms in our home had no heat to be sure not to warp these treasures.

My mother, Shirley Greenfield, rescued antique dolls in disarray and restored them, not to as-new perfection, but as if they'd been played with for years and had become faded and worn through love and time. This experience was my gateway to the "beauty of imperfection" aesthetic that's at the core of what I do now. Mum's dolls had personality and real soul, and collectors came to my mum's booth in Camden Passage knowing that soul is what they would find, along with her welcoming ability to listen and share stories. The community of doll collectors is unique, and they all have their reasons to be attracted to dolls. Storytelling came with the territory. Sometimes, on Saturdays, mum would have me "hold the fort" while she visited fellow vendors and even at my tender preteen age I took on my mum's ability to listen to the journeys and stories of customers. Of course, I also knew the backstory of most of the dolls, and sometimes I made a sale. I wasn't academic, so the market became my place of learning, where I absorbed the process of trading from beginning to end: buying dolls, restoring them to be ready for reloving, and making a profit along the way.

CLOCKWISE FROM TOP LEFT: *My mum in New Zealand as a young girl, wearing a dress she made. Me, wearing a sailor dress made by my mum. Me with my son Jake, relaxed on the first slipcover I ever had made. My rosy cheeks and my mum's love. Clutching Simon, my bear. Me and my sister, Deborah, with my parents sometime in the 1960s, in Forest Hills, Queens. Jake, my daughter Lily, and me; a happy beach trio. Lily, head-to-toe in mud, used to a home of washable furniture. A picture of joy: me, wearing a coat mum made for me, playing tug-of-war.*

the market life

Going to various London markets with Mum and Dad made me aware of their different processes of shopping, and this was my training ground. Catching up with Dad was often my mission—he was always rushing ahead, and I couldn't understand why he wasn't sauntering up and down the aisles, chatting to people and browsing like my mum; but it was actually observing him that inspired my pace and process for the way I shop now. He could edit a tower of books with a glance. He knew how to seek out treasures even if they were in a soggy cardboard box under a table. I, too, have an uncanny sixth sense about where to seek, dig for, and rescue treasures. I can look out at rows of stalls and piles of stuff, and my eyes know how to edit through and when to stop and rummage.

For my mother, it was more about the spiritual gleanings of the marketplace: the conversations about where this came from and where you found that; the hunt for scraps of silk and velvet, or ribbons and buttons in which she could see potential, and at the same time appreciate that a faded bow or broken necklace was once precious enough to someone that they thought it worth passing on rather than throwing out. Over time she also formed many meaningful friendships where conversations surpassed anything to do with dolls.

I was probably about ten or eleven when I would go with them, torn between my racing-around dad and my gathering history along with treasures mum. I'm now a combination of both. Twice a year I plant myself for several weeks at my B&B, The Prairie, near the Round Top Antique Fairs, in Texas, during which I have the luxury of time,

so I can search for both treasures and stories. My intuition, along with my familiarity with the vendors, guides me to the best treasures while picking up tales along the way. The heat of Texas makes people shop at a slower pace than the rain-soaked flea market of Kempton Park in London (always top of my list on Tuesdays when I'm in the UK), where the rain and wind force you to pick up your pace.

My parents, of course, were looking for small things that could be carried home in bags, so they didn't have to establish pick-up points, and deal with trucks and all the other logistics I have to consider. But I still shop with the same ethos. My mum had a handbag full of envelopes and plastic bags, some for cash, some for receipts, like a portable filing system. Hers was a very simple business: she paid cash for everything, her overhead was next to nothing, and a small profit kept her in business for many years enabling her to contribute greatly to supporting our family. At the beginning, my business model was based on hers, as that was all I knew: to buy what I could afford, be frugal with overhead, and add a small profit to ensure a solid business.

There is a term in our industry for people who frequent flea markets, antique shows, and estate and car boot sales, getting to know what vendors are looking for: they're called pickers. Mum and Dad both had pickers, who from time to time would call on them and sometimes come to our home to deliver books or dolls. I remember these transactions vividly, listening to the stories, the questions, and the price negotiations, and then Mum going to find her precious envelopes, hidden somewhere in the house, to retrieve her cash. I, too, now have an array of pickers!

It seems I have been searching for treasures for a very long time...

LEFT: *Wedding table set up in the barn of The Prairie, my bed-and-breakfast: flea market finds all come together with their wonkiness, flaky paint, and perfect mismatches.*

RIGHT: *Shopping for more imperfect treasures.*

Me, my mum, and my sister, Deborah, in Southampton, setting out on our QEI transatlantic crossing to the USA.

our voyage to america

My mum was from New Zealand, my dad from Chicago, but although his entire life was spent in England, Dad was an American at heart, and to this day he loves hot dogs and the Chicago Cubs. My parents met in England in their early thirties, both somewhat bohemian, neither settling for conventional careers or proper jobs. They both had an array of different types of work, and I'd say we were raised modestly in an atmosphere of creativity.

When I was about four, Dad and Mum thought it would benefit the family to move to America, so we sailed the QE1 from Southampton to New York. We had normal tickets, but it seems we were quite cute as a family, with my sister Deborah and me dressed in mum's hand-sewn couture; for whatever reason we were upgraded to a very glamorous suite, which is one of my earliest memories of a chic environment. We adopted an American life for about four years: I remember hot summers, sprinklers on lawns, going to summer day-camps, and more freedom to play in the streets than we'd ever had in London, partly due to the weather but also to the way the neighborhoods were set up with cul-de-sacs and alleyways. Mum worked part-time for a fashion house, hand-sewing and cutting patterns. My dad taught French and, lost in his academic world, was a bit of a recluse. After a few years, we didn't find our fortune, so we flew back to the UK, returning to a tiny flat in North London where Mum and Dad entered their different worlds of antique dealership.

an education in imperfection

My room was tiny, a box room, really (that's British English for a storeroom) but though it was small, it was where big dreams and ideas were planted. And it was where I began my world of make-believe, adventure, and observation of life. I have such fond memories of looking out my window onto our very ordinary street, watching for the early morning milk delivery cart. I favored the days Mum ordered the gold cap milk bottle, the creamiest of them all. Those days represented decadence to me (this was well before the days of organic skimmed milk). Once a month the "rag & bone" cart would trundle down the street calling out for junk, and on Sundays the Salvation Army would march down the street, singing songs of glory and pride. I recall one day our street was transformed into a movie set for a B movie. I was at my window, transfixed, watching for "lights, camera, action!" This awoke my curiosity about the magic of Hollywood and made me determined to one day try to make it my world.

Our flat was furnished with secondhand finds and a few new elements, artfully pulled together by Mum—there was nothing shiny in our orbit, but Mum was a whiz with a paintbrush. She loved to transform unfinished pine furniture with transparent paint stains of reds, purples, and yellows. But she could also climb up a ladder and fix our roof and do the plumbing. She set a high benchmark for a good work ethic and a "can do" attitude.

My mum was both creative and practical. She was frugal but didn't cut corners on attention to detail. She often made clothes for my sister and me. I used to love the onset of spring, as it meant our navy wool school uniforms would be put away and pretty pale yellow spring gingham dresses, handmade by Mum, would have their time. It meant daffodils were soon to bloom. I loved the character and imperfections of a handmade dress. I loved the humility of the sewing; I loved the treasure of those dresses.

Our home exuded culture, art, and creativity. Painting, reading, playing piano and violin, and studying ballet, along with tending to a teeny back garden, which my mum tended to herself, set the stage for the storytelling that would become such a vital part of my world. It was here that Mum started exploring the idea of restoring and selling dolls as a business from a booth in Camden Passage—a long-established London antique emporium with a scruffy and upmarket end. Mum always felt more comfortable on the scruffy side of the tracks. Little by little she began to gather and restore—in her own special imperfect way—and soon established herself as a focal point for dealers and collectors. Her dolls were not precious, but in her hands they had beauty, and quality, and, thanks to her restoration skills, they could be handled and didn't have to sit stiffly in a display cabinet. A big-time doll dealer had a fancy shop at the grand end of the market, and I remember going in and feeling intimidated by the untouchable perfection. The Beauty of Imperfection was in my blood.

The beauty of imperfection: A flea market–found sideboard with crackled patina, faded paint, and petals falling. Such evidence of life and love are hard to fake and are priceless.

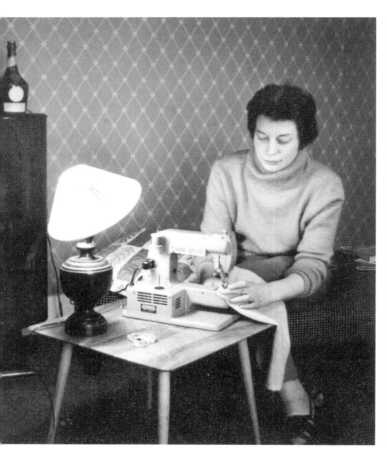

*Three generations of creativity: My mum
sewing by a wonky light; me, in my creative
world; and Lily, studying her work at a fitting.*

Mum's restoration system was unique, with a method to the chaos in her workroom. There were boxes overflowing with fabric scraps, porcelain heads, limbs, wigs, and glass eyeballs (a little gruesome)—and the macabre tools of strung-out wire hangers and string she used to hook arms and legs together through the torso. I have a warm memory of seeing light under her door while she was in there all alone making magic, putting Humpty Dumpty together again. I look around my small, overstuffed workroom now: boxes of fabric swatches, scraps of bits and bobs, chandelier drops, and silk flowers. And even though my stores are thought to be part of an empire, and fancy to a certain degree, it is my embracing of the beauty of imperfection that still makes my stores inviting. The Shabby component brings humility to the Chic.

I have always loved the fantasy of the crown jewels.

hollywood dreams

We weren't a touchy-feely family. Mum was quite busy with her business and raising two girls, and Dad was an intellectual recluse. Our house had an attic with a trapdoor and ladder, and I have many memories of Dad scuttling up it and watching his feet disappearing through the trapdoor, and then the feeling of excitement when I saw the door open again. A bond my father and I did share was our love of the old black-and-white Hollywood movies shown on the BBC on Sunday afternoons at 3 p.m. *Gone with the Wind*, *The Wizard of Oz*, *Sunset Boulevard*, and anything starring Marilyn Monroe were firm favorites. I cherished these times. The Hollywood magic got to me and sparked my interest in the world of storytelling, make-believe, props, costumes, and sets. It was an interest I shared with my childhood friend Sophie Muller, and on sleepovers we'd dream of "making it in Hollywood." She still lives in London but travels often to Hollywood and is now one of the top video directors in the world. So we did make it, both of us, in our own indirect ways.

I was madly keen to find a way into the entertainment industry, but I had no contacts, and I needed to earn a living. When I first left home, I was just sixteen—I worked briefly as an au pair in North London; I lived in a grim council flat in Islington with a damp bathroom shared with other flats, where I needed to put money in the meter for hot water. To this day I am frugal with hot water! Through a local employment agency I found an administrative job working for Warner Brothers in London's Soho. It sounded glamorous, but my job was to manually count stubs for ticket sales for the whole country. I felt somewhat connected to that shiny world out there, but in reality I was merely sitting at a desk, counting tickets. So back at the employment agency I found a job as a receptionist for a commercial production company in Covent Garden. My job was to answer the phones, buy the sandwiches, and restock the bar.

I threw myself into the job, and my bosses really enjoyed me, as I was willing and curious. On occasion, I was allowed to go to the set to see a commercial being shot, and it was here that I met the costume designer Shuna Harwood. We struck up a rapport, and when I finally left my job it was to assist her with work on commercials as needed. So my days of being employed full-time ended at seventeen years old, but I was chipping away at the world I wanted to be in.

Little by little I got more freelance work, first as a junior photographic stylist and then, when I was still seventeen, as the head stylist for a fashion shoot at Disney World, in Florida, for F.W. Woolworth's. This was the game-changer. I went to Florida with some very ordinary clothes and models, but it could have been a shoot for the cover of *Vogue*, as far as I was concerned. I was in charge, I saw my first palm tree, and I spent two weeks at the happiest place on earth. I felt what it was like to be free; when I got back to London, I just couldn't settle. I had a boyfriend at the time—a jolly, roughish antique dealer—but something in my wiring was telling me it was time to explore. I needed to make a break for it and to get back to the land of opportunity.

I saved up a little money and sought out some contacts: my father had a sort of cousin none of us had ever met who lived in Los Angeles, and my boyfriend's best friend's sister lived there. Armed with these phone numbers and my thin portfolio, I made my voyage. It was a very brave move for an essentially shy person, but I was determined. In those days, when you didn't come from money, the decision to move 6,000 miles away from home was a big deal, but my parents had moved about as life took them, and so it didn't seem unnatural to me. My mum moved to London from New Zealand, my dad from Chicago, and now my son has moved to London from Los Angeles, so it seems a gypsy spirit is bred in the bones of our family.

finding my way

I was able to stay with my cousin for a couple of weeks. She lived in Beverly Hills, with lots of formica, a very fancy big pale blue boat of a Cadillac, drinks cabinets, manicures, and hairdresser appointments. She and her husband were also members of a yacht club where I went a couple of times. I had no idea such abundance and fanciness existed. I was this young, scruffy, boho English girl, and I think they were fascinated by me. I had saved enough money to buy an orange convertible—I was yet to finesse my palette—and I was thrilled with the mobility.

I set goals to achieve my dream of getting into "the biz." Every day I methodically called dozens of potential contacts in the LA411, a directory for the film and photography industry. Well before emailing a resume was protocol, the only way to sell yourself was with a proper phone call followed by an interview. Eventually I got an English cockney guy on the phone, keen to give a chance to a fellow Brit. With my Thomas Brothers map in hand, I was set for my first interview. I arrived at an ominous building with armed security guards at the door. I'd never seen a security guard before, never mind a gun, and in the lobby there were girls floating about in lingerie. Innocently and unbeknownst to me, I'd arrived at the headquarters of a rather risqué magazine—shy, blushing, modest, naïve Rachel Greenfield. What was I walking into?

The English guy on the phone seemed both impressed with my fledgling portfolio and understanding of my plight—a foreigner trying to get started. But as much as I was excited by the potential break, I knew I didn't want to be around that world, so I said I'd pull the sets together as long as I didn't have to be at the shoots. By the end of the interview, we had negotiated a substantial daily fee and I had in my hand drive-on passes to the 20th Century Fox and Universal Studios prop rooms: the back lot keys to Hollywood. I was ecstatic. I worked there for just a little a while, getting experience in pulling room sets and costumes together to create make-believe. I remember making a bunker from the Vietnam War, and my swan song being a version of *The Little House on the Prairie*, which is ironic as now I have my own wholesome Shabby Chic Prairie. By this time I'd been in America for several months, networking with the growing English community of filmmakers. I met Bobbie Read, a lovely and talented costume designer who took me under her wing. As her assistant I worked with a group of English directors who were transitioning from commercials into movies. We did commercials with the likes of Tony Scott and Adrian Lyne. Budgets were huge and there was plenty of work, as the talent of the British was much in demand. Bobbie Read and I collaborated often on period costume commercials, which added to my lessons from Mum on using innovative fabric treatments to give the illusion of authentic timeworn age.

I was on my way. I got my first little apartment in Hollywood on one of those blocks that look like rundown motels with dank, yucky swimming pools surrounded by unloved palm trees. But through my rose-colored glasses, I had a beautiful turquoise pool surrounded by tropical foliage, and on the weekend I could drive to the beach in my orange convertible and life was amazing. Every Saturday I'd cover myself in Johnson's baby oil and fry down at Santa Monica beach. These were my young, fun years, but I was very responsible, always wanting to take the next step in my career, driven partly by the anxiety of wanting to feel financially safe. I loved the work, and I loved being part of a team and working with creative people.

Later, I rented a rundown shabby house in the Hollywood Hills with four guys. This was the beginning of my white period. I decided to paint everything, including the floors—crazy because I was living with guys who didn't know the meaning of the word clean, and the bathroom fluctuated from gross to gorgeous. But the place looked amazing—a white WOW!

My first ever Shabby Chic sofa in my first ever store: faded beauty and elegance, with an array of eclectic decorative pillows; many subtle details of ruffles, pleats, and floppy lace adorn faded velvet and silk taffeta.

Lily, Jake and me. RIGHT: *On my wedding day, with a floppy lace bow in my hair.*

Around this time I was working doing costumes on a Pan Am commercial campaign where the idea was to re-create the famous Clipper service. As it was to be shown in many different countries, we reshot the opening with a spokesperson for each different country; the ad agency brought in a director from each country for that section. It was a wonderful job—we had to re-create all the uniforms and clothes for the passengers right down to the last detail. I spent weeks in the wardrobe departments of the major studios. The Clio Award-winning director David Ashwell was chosen for the English version.

We struck up a friendship and over the next year and a half our friendship grew; eventually we got married. It was a modest ceremony in Kings Cross, London, well before the concept of a "Shabby Chic Wedding" was even a dream.

David's creative process was different from mine. He hand-drew beautiful, meticulous storyboards, thinking through every frame of his story. My way of working was much more spontaneous, but I learned a lot from his methodology. I don't have his skill set to draw, but my mind is where my storytelling starts. We began our married life together in Hollywood, but when I was pregnant with Lily, every smell made me throw up, so the idea of open spaces and the breeze of beach living was appealing—thus began my love affair with Malibu, which back then was a lovely low-key community of shabby shacks, perfect for young families with the ocean as their garden. It was the first home for Lily, and two years later, Jake. My husband had four other children from prior marriages who would visit from London from time to time, so the house was pretty busy. As the reality of sticky fingers and sandy feet leaving their marks on my furnishings set in, I was determined not to become a neurotic mum with "child-free zones" in the house, and so began the process of designing a "kid friendly" home without compromising the golden rule: beauty, comfort, and function.

I had vague memories of slipcovers being a mainstay in English country homes, so I began to research getting some. I called every upholsterer in the yellow pages, but the only offerings available were plastic covers. I soon realized my vision didn't really exist: I wanted a machine-washable, preshrunk slipcover, custom-made for my sofa. So I decided to design one and get it made. After a lot of experimenting with fabrics and sewing, my first slipcover was born...and soon many of my friends wanted them too.

*A cherished old Polaroid of Lily and Jake
with early signs of Shabby Chic decor.*

RIGHT: *A casual artwork of ballet shoes,
and my sister, Deborah, a professional dancer.*

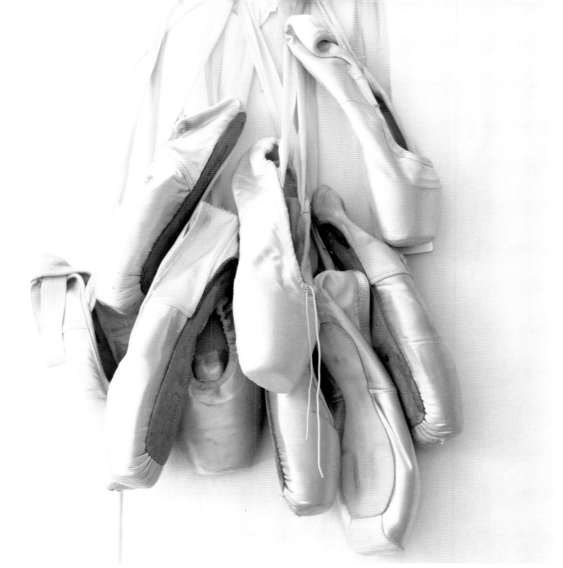

following my heart and reinventing the slipcover

Unfortunately, my marriage lasted only a few years, and the kids were still tiny when we separated. Earning a living and having a creative outlet was important to me. I wanted to be my own boss, juggle the kids, continue with storytelling, and use the talents I had picked up along the way. The idea of having a shop ticked all the boxes.

As I formulated my idea, the name "Slips" came to mind because slipcovers were to be the core of my store. Then one day David and I were leafing though a magazine and came across an article, I think referring to a castle, describing the décor as being both shabby and chic. It was quite clear that my shop had to be called Shabby Chic, such a perfect description of what I do, and a perfect definition of my brand. "Slips" was quickly changed to Shabby Chic. I made no adjustment to my designs and products, only to the hand-stamped hangtags and my sign on the door.

When my husband and I separated, I moved to Santa Monica, down the Pacific Coast Highway from Malibu, where I found a store on Montana Avenue. There were more obvious locations that would have been far more conducive to the home-furnishing industry, but it was a neighborhood street with grocery stores, dry cleaners, and other conveniences. I went into it in all innocence. I didn't do studies of foot traffic or price points, and I knew nothing of cash flows and inventories. All I had was my vision, the story I wanted to tell, a hunch for what I felt was a gap in the home-furnishing market, and a bit of training from my mum and dad.

PREVIOUS PAGE: *Traditional lines of a sofa, made softer with a pink slipcover and the bling of a signature chandelier.*

ABOVE: *A modern, oversize sofa made inviting with a rumpled canvas slipcover.* RIGHT: *It's all about ruffles in the ballroom.*

The location felt like the right place to be, and my instincts were right because I'm still there twenty-five years later, albeit after a few bumps in the road (including an earthquake and a brief going-out-of-business time). The slipcovers were to be the platform of my business, the revolutionary step. But I also filled the shop with my storytelling, gathering vintage accessories and furnishings, sourced the only way I knew how, from flea markets. I collected lamps, rugs, mirrors, coffee tables, cupboards, and small accessories. At that time, I only purchased things that needed a dust off and confident presentation, as I didn't have the set-up to do restoration, but little by little I put together a larger repertoire from which to create my stories. Fortunately, my house had a garage, so this acted as my first distribution center, where I stored inventory to be shipped out as needed. My soon-to-be-ex-husband lent me money to open the store. But because of the way I was planning to find my goods, and my generally frugal way of making do, I didn't need a lot of money. I simply purchased what I could afford if I knew I could sell it later.

I opened Shabby Chic in the summer of 1989. It was about 1,000 square feet. Over the years, two adjoining stores became available, so today we sit on 3000 square feet. I sorted out the back room as a place I could plop the kids if needed, and initially hired one salesgirl, Stephanie. Shabby Chic was an instant hit. People popped by for a peek and found themselves mesmerized by my little world. I hadn't thought through what to do if sales were strong. I didn't understand you had to have inventory in the pipes, and I didn't have anyone I could call to order more stock of my vintage accessories, so most Sundays at around 6 a.m. I would head to a local flea market with Jake and Lily in my double stroller trying to replenish as quickly as I could. My children were on the receiving end of many "just a few more minutes" gifts of rusty lunch boxes and used Barbie dolls that I would buy for them as I shopped for treasures for the store. Over the next weeks and months, I quickly learned the furniture business: researching, learning the ropes, and building up an address book full of pattern cutters, furniture manufacturers, and sewers. I didn't really know what I was doing, but I stayed focused on my story. I worked hard and kept things simple. I'd struck a chord, word spread, and I learned how to run a business, one sofa at a time.

Making Shabby Chic, Again

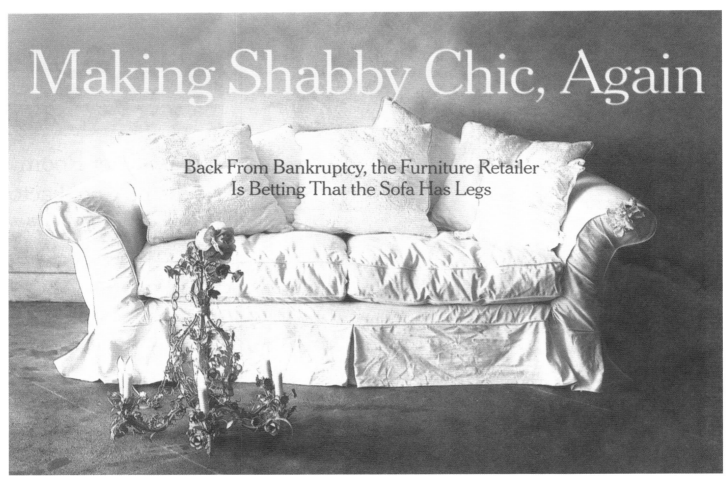

Back From Bankruptcy, the Furniture Retailer Is Betting That the Sofa Has Legs

Hollywood

"Trays of food are loving gestures"

sometimes known in the London lounges of Ladbroke Grove as "chakra" (Remember Sada from *Big Brother 2000*: "I believe that everything happens the way it is meant to happen. I also believe that change is a prerequisite to happiness. We steer our own destiny.")

Alternatively, there is the Rob Lowe approach. After examining Sting and Trudie's faded decor, the Hollywood heart-throb went home to construct an exact replica of their interior design.

Nonetheless, untangling ourselves from one's fringed scarves for a moment, it is easy to see that the return of indoor shabbiness makes

Jennifer Lopez: riding the vanguard of shabby interior fashion

shabby chic was meant to be

Over the years I have been asked many times to define the components that made Shabby Chic such a success. And as I think about it, the main reason was a combination of my innovative merchandise (the machine-washable slipcovered sofa), and how I presented my world. Every item in my store had a backstory and a purpose—the mushy sofas looked as if someone had just left the room for a moment; the gorgeously inviting beds were rumpled like someone had just gotten up. My heart and soul were layered into my stories, and they resonated with people.

The "westside" street I chose by chance was in a neighborhood many celebrities had started to move to, on the run from Beverly Hills. Madonna, Bruce Willis, Gwyneth Paltrow, and Brad Pitt all ended up in my store, and this at a time well before camera phones and aggressive paparazzi. Celebrities value their privacy when it comes to their homes, so when the likes of Bruce Springsteen bought something, I honored confidentiality. Still, word wv that there was a new movement called Shabby Chic.

My store was also full of ideas and inspirations. I was able to offer a vision and products for people who wanted to find furnishings but who also wanted to make them their own, with their own stories.

Over the next year or two I educated myself about furniture manufacturers, learned what makes a good chair and a good slipcover, and came to understand the importance of a good pattern cutter. I experimented endlessly with different fabrics to see how much they shrank, puckered, or faded. I was partial to soft cushions, so the formula of how much down to feather to foam took some working out, too. Over time, I built up a production department and mastered the art of knowing how much

of what to order. Understanding inventory, cash flow, and sales goals were lessons along the way, and continue to be so. In those early days, it was about having a good pen and some graph paper; now it's all about the best computer program. There have been good years and bad years, and I have concluded that being successful is about making constant adjustments and finding reliable vendors and employees. While it's lovely to build long-term relationships, life happens and new relationships are always needed.

One day Tom Cohen, a New York businessman, came in to the Santa Monica store and introduced me to the idea of opening a store in New York. I'm not sure what I was thinking, with a baby and a toddler, and my first store not yet six months old, but ignorance can be bliss. Brendan McBreen had come on board to manage the Santa Monica store and we had a couple of other employees. I was juggling the babies and keeping up with learning the needs of the store, so I couldn't physically up and move to New York, but we were quickly becoming a team. I secured a bank loan, one of my newly employed associates, Dara Schneider, jumped at the opportunity to relocate; she and I, with some guidance from Tom, opened store number two in New York in the fall of 1989.

From a marketing standpoint it was a brilliant strategic move to suddenly be a national bicoastal company, although it wasn't strategy on my part, just a "why not" philosophy. As I wasn't educated in business or economics, I never understood why I couldn't do something I wanted to do. In my ignorance I was able to make decisions unencumbered by too much information—just a couple of envelopes and a check book, and it worked.

I have always been fortunate to receive meaningful press about Shabby Chic, about me, and about my celebrity clients. In the early days this was how news of the "Shabby Chic Movement" spread from coast to coast in the days before Google and social media. We continued to make positive headlines, including when Shabby Chic made its comeback in 2009.

evolving, growing, and finding my voice

My business has had a natural evolution rather than a strategy. In the early days, for every store I opened I took out a $100,000 loan to buy inventory and security for the lease. This left me with working capital to tide me over for about three months. I don't like debt; it doesn't sit well with me. So I always started to pay down loans from the day I opened my doors. Banks could see my process and were always ready to lend me more for each new store.

Dara Schneider, who relocated to the store in New York, did the same when we opened in Chicago and San Francisco, and we were a good team. Somehow I muddled through most of the business as well as the creative sides and she handled more of the operations while juggling the multiple locations. In a totally non-strategic way, Shabby Chic was becoming a big little empire. I was enjoying the modest and organic growth, but in time Dara and I realised we had different goals for our lives and the company, and our relationship had run its course.

We had neglected to write down legally what our relationship was, so the best we could come up with was a muddled separation: she took the New York and San Francisco stores, I took the Chicago (the least successful) and Santa Monica stores, along with my beloved trademarked name, Shabby Chic, so I could continue to grow. By not wanting to confront the situation and negotiate a cleaner split, many years of confusion were caused as to whether the New York and San Francisco stores were the true Shabby Chic or not.

Meanwhile, I went on to open two more stores, have my own TV shows, write my books, and find wonderful license partners in Target and Marks & Spencer. I also ventured into the wholesale business. I started to understand the word margin, the amount of profit between the cost of goods and retail prices. Some products I could make economically enough that I could sell them to other stores and they would still make a profit when they were sold. I enjoyed this, as it was during a time that a lot of small Mom and Pop stores were opening; and I liked the community.

Shabby Chic has had several logos and brand extension names over the years. With a Champagne taste but a beer budget for marketing tools, I have always cared deeply about the smallest details.

CLOCKWISE FROM TOP LEFT: *Shabby Chic Furnishings rubber stamp, c. 1989. Embroidered nametape for bedding, c. 1999. Rachel Ashwell Shabby Chic—dye cut, burnished, metallic—very expensive and fancy (when budgets allowed), c. 2007. Rachel Ashwell Couture label for our prom dresses, silk-screened on linen, c. 2006. Chic soap boxes. Simple silver hangtag (when budgets were tight), c. 2009, and still in use. Simply Shabby Chic, our Target logo, inspired by a back stamp on a vintage plate, 2004.*

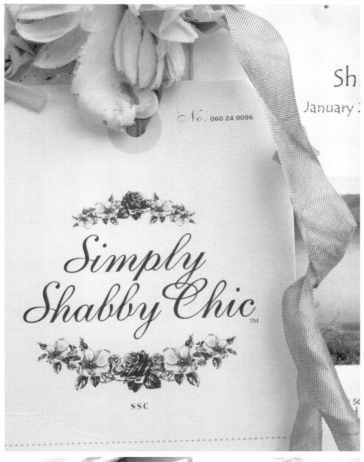

As simple as they seemed, Shabby Chic T-shirt sheets
were one of the most difficult of products to develop:
finding looms big enough to knit jersey sheets, and
sewing machines that could keep straight lines on
a stretchy fabric took a long while to perfect.

oprah, tv, and books

I had never planned on having a TV show or writing books. The combination of being quite shy and uneducated didn't have me setting those types of goals. However, when I happened to meet Judith Regan, a prominent New York publisher, she saw how my Shabby Chic world could translate into book form. The opportunity for a TV show came from the Style Network and, like so many times before, I thought, "Why not?" The world is such a different place now, with social media and the internet, but back in the day, I was very fortunate to have these platforms to spread the word about Shabby Chic. I do believe I have been blessed with opportunity, but I also credit myself with working hard and I am grateful for finding my passion. I always say working hard, and finding your passion and the right team, are the vital components to success.

My TV show Rachel Ashwell's Shabby Chic on Style, reached all corners of the globe, and it's interesting to me how well-loved my fifty-four episodes were. It was well before the advent of reality TV, but my shows were my reality—I did walk my talk. The shows were often shot in my home, with my kids in the background, and were pretty, practical, and authentic.

My wholesale opportunity exploded one year thanks to Oprah. I had gone on her show as a guest to promote my book Shabby Chic Treasure Hunting, and as a thank-you gift I sent her a set of the Shabby Chic T-shirt sheets I had just developed. She and her producers loved them, and they were featured on the show "Oprah's 20 Favorite Things." Amazingly, the segment for my sheets was her telling Sylvester Stallone all about them and that was it! Shabby Chic store phones rang off the hook with thousands of people wanting the sheets. The good news was I got more orders than I knew what to do with; the bad news was I couldn't possibly fill all the orders. The bad news was also that a few of the "big players," who could react quicker than me, knocked-off the sheets and sold them cheaper than I ever could. On the upside, Shabby Chic was growing into a lifestyle brand as well as the famous slipcover company and we got credit for being the mother of invention.

So my empire grew, but the question about whether I owned the New York and San Francisco stores always hung heavy.

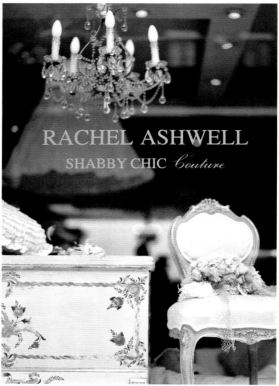

As retail has changed over the years, the experience of pretty little shops and meaningful customer service is a rare but appreciated one. I still love nothing more than visiting one of my stores, fluffing pillows, meeting customers, and spending time with my Shabby Chic family of sales associates.

change and lessons

Over the years, for different reasons, I explored the idea of selling all or part of Shabby Chic, and on the way I had some interesting encounters with wise businesspeople. One of the most important to me was with Harold Shultz of Starbucks, who wrote a book called *Pour Your Heart Into It: How Starbucks Built a Company One Cup at a Time.* I found it helpful to learn how he faced his challenges while striving to meet his goals and maintain his values. As a thank-you I sent him one of my books, and shortly thereafter we met, for talk and tea (as I don't drink coffee). One of his pieces of advice that I treasure to this day: "Whatever you decide to do, or not to do, make sure you look back at what you've done." Being as driven as I am, these words are important for me to remember. Over the years, when I have needed advice, he is someone I treasure and can call upon.

By 2007, the economy was pretty flush, and I thought I'd explore what could come next for Shabby. My children had gone off to college, and in a metaphoric way, I thought it was time for Shabby to do the same. Up to this point, I had hand-held Shabby Chic as I had my children, and to get to the next level, I had to explore letting go and making space for those who knew more about how to take it to the next level. Creatively, I felt I'd plateaued, and I was now stuck on the business side.

It's always a tricky balance when you own your own company to know how much money to reinvest and when to borrow, what type of money to go after and how much to grow. Bigger isn't always better. I talked to a few investment banker types, all rather out of my league as far as understanding debt, equity, return on money. All I knew was my envelope filing system and how to acquire simple bank loans. In the end I settled on Goode Partners to be my investors. They were young but seemingly experienced in the retail world, I felt they understood what I was about, and they were very patient and flexible with me during the process of deciding how much of a percentage I wanted to sell. My priority was to have control, at least what I understood that to mean, so I sold a minority stake. It's what is called a "debt equity" deal, where there is cash and also some debt layered in by leveraging against the value of the company. With the cash infusion we were finally able to buy back my beloved New York and San Francisco stores. We then had six stores, some licensing deals, and a small wholesale business: the company was clean and steady. I was ready to surrender the business side of things to those who knew more than I did, so I could focus on the magic of creativity with the security of my little nest egg.

boom and bust

The focus of Goode Partners was retail expansion, while still supporting our licence program of Simply Shabby Chic at Target. Their plan was to open fifty-seven stores over five years—quite an undertaking. Producing and shipping furniture is a cumbersome business, but they were confident and I trusted their strategic planning. My role was the creative vision and the design work. When I saw the inventory we were taking on, the huge warehousing spaces, the computer systems, and the growing "Dream Team" of vice presidents and CEOs, my gut started to churn a bit because I couldn't quite understand where the sales were coming from to support the growing overhead. Up until that point, I had had an array of associates working with me at different levels in the world of Shabby Chic. Some lasted for many years; some associations were more fleeting. My business was complex and forever evolving, and it took people who were able to "go with the flow." Unlike with my flea market treasures, I didn't always know what I was looking for in a business associate. Sometimes I could have used a better flashlight.

I'm quite frugal with my remodels, and the six stores I had were in charming, wonky buildings very suited to the Shabby and Chic merchandise. But when you plan to open fifty-seven stores, they're not all going to be in charming old buildings—some are going to be in shiny new malls and these are expensive to fit out and rent. As we began taking on store after store, I started to feel really disconnected. I didn't know how to create the Shabby Chic I knew in these bright shiny palaces of commerce. I'd always been able to create my stories fairly well, but I need good bones: texture from old walls, creaks from floor boards, natural light through street level stores—atmosphere that was quite hard to achieve in new buildings. Because I was, and still am, the only vintage buyer I couldn't keep up with the inventory needs as we approached even fifteen stores, so we started compromising by buying a larger percentage of stock from the open market and pick-up items that started to feel a bit too mainstream. Elements of Shabby Chic were beginning to blend into other brands, and we were losing our magic.

The logistics weren't working either. We had to deal with expensive freight errors like sofas destined for Albuquerque ending up in Boston two weeks late. All of that was going on and I was working in an environment I wasn't used to with people I didn't know. Had sales continued to be strong maybe we could have ridden out the storm and grown into the compromised design, but we, along with everyone else, were hit with the 2008–2009 economic downturn, which hit especially hard in the home market. I still question how my original stores would have functioned if I hadn't done the expansion. I ran a tight ship and was frugal, so maybe we could have survived. The Goode guys and I really liked one another; we tried to slow down and get out of some leases, but it was a perfect storm and it all fell apart quickly. In two months, November 2008 to January 2009, Shabby Chic sank like the Titanic.

The dismantling was so sad. We were closing stores, one at a time, in the hope of saving the others. It was the long, expensive leases in the big shiny malls that were the biggest burden. From December to August 2009, as the stores closed down, the banks got involved and brought liquidators in to sell everything down to my personal treasures and the pencils on the desks. By this time, most of the "Dream Team" had gone elsewhere, except for Jaimee Seabury. She had been brought on as a head buyer, but when it all went south she jumped in with everything she had to try to save whatever could be saved. The hardest part for me was the scavenger mentality that comes with the process of liquidation. There was such sadness, but still lines of people shopping, because they knew this was their last chance to buy Shabby Chic. And it was very difficult for staff members who had to help in the sell-off that was ultimately going to sink them. I met one liquidator boss who appeared to have compassion; it was evident that it pained him to sell off the ruffly prom dress from my office. It was a Sunday and the liquidators were strategizing how they were going to take over the stores. I asked if I could design the sell-off signs in pink, so at least the stores went down looking pretty. He wisely told me that customers had to believe Shabby Chic was going out of business and only the official harsh orange and black signs could send that signal. I knew it was over. I never visited a store with the ugly black and orange signs.

So that was it. Twinkle lights out, one by one. But at the same time, I couldn't run away. I was burdened with the legal aspects of going out of business: stacks and stacks of agreements, contracts, spreadsheets, layoffs—by now my dream job had become my worst nightmare. I had lost my mum in October 2008, a few months before the unraveling of Shabby Chic. In a way I am grateful she didn't live to see its demise, as she loved it so. But I did have a grieving father to attend to, so with my emotions churning and everything sold off, including my beloved name, I headed back to London. While it was a hard time for our family, with much uncertainty and many tears from me, there were definitely lessons of humility: things in life happen, unexpectedly and often unfairly, but it is how we step through those times that is the true test of character.

Sometimes things go wonky, but beauty is rarely far away.

picking up the pieces

Selling off tangible things is easier than selling a name. Even though Shabby Chic was an international brand name, it was so intertwined with me that the bank had a tricky time selling it for the best price possible unless I came along too. I tried to stay on board and work through the complicated negotiations, but my nerves and emotions were pretty frayed from all that had gone on. It felt like getting into an arranged marriage to someone you didn't know when you were still in love with your previous partner. Dealing with contracts and lawyers was my reality for the longest time, and I was worried my creativity would be lost forever as the other side of my brain was forced to navigate the quagmire.

With everything sold off, the new owner of the trademark name Shabby Chic had more interest in licensing opportunities than in the retail business, as in his eyes the risk of leases and buying inventory was too great, especially in the new economic world of 2009. But creating a licensing platform for a brand is always easier if there is the presence of a store to help tell the story. And my beloved stores were gone.

During this process, some of my long-standing employees found other opportunities for themselves. But I did have a small core that stood by me and Shabby and, led by Jaimee Seabury, helped navigate a new day, even on days when I couldn't see the way. The new owner and I worked out terms where I would be given the rights to reopen some stores under the name Rachel Ashwell Shabby Chic Couture, and I would also support the creative component of the licensing arm of Shabby Chic.

I had to find a way to slip into the ball gown again, metaphorically speaking.

Finding affordable locations was not difficult as, at the time, retail in general was falling apart. In the end, I re-opened my Santa Monica store right back where it used to be; the New York store moved around the corner from the old location, and for the first time ever, I put a stake in the ground of my home country and opened a precious little store in Notting Hill, London. I had loads of non-competes in my contract for a few years but under my agreement I was randomly allowed to open hotels so that's how my innocent Little House on the Prairie (The Prairie by Rachel Ashwell) bed and breakfast came into being. It was a proud day when we got onto the Condé Nast Traveler list of Top New Hotels.

It was becoming obvious that the new brand owner and I were pulling in different directions and had different priorities, which made for a wonky whole. My stores, the birth of The Prairie, and my books continued to be the inspiration for the brand and created a dynamic for the licensing group, including the Simply Shabby Chic partnership with Target, which thrived. While both the retail and licensing sides succeeded during those years, it was challenging to have two different leaders. In this day and age, any specialist retail business needs the profitability of a license platform to supplement the expense of running the business, and a license platform needs the allure of a retail store to tell and sell the story: it became apparent the company needed to be made whole again. And so I did some deep soul-searching as to whether I had it in me financially and emotionally to regroup and rekindle the pieces of Shabby Chic. I asked myself what was driving my desire: Was it ego or personal identity? In time the answer came to me: I simply love Shabby Chic. While I had a small but strong "village" behind me, I didn't want to entertain new financial partners. I had to buy the brand back. So I put my hands in my pockets, we rolled up our sleeves and made some decisions . . . It was time for the world of Shabby Chic to come home to me.

LEFT: *The hand-painted sign at the entrance of our little bit of heaven, The Prairie.*

ABOVE: *I have always felt at home in nature, in my world of make-believe.*

at the heart of shabby chic

Shabby Chic is a manifestation of all that I love, all that I understand, and the rules and values I grew up with. Over the years I have fine-tuned my art and evolved my aesthetic, but the same principles remain as true as they always were: Beauty, comfort, and fuction and the beauty of imperfection.

When Shabby Chic first opened its doors, people looking to furnish their homes only had the choice of department stores, with a vast collection of middle-of-the-road offerings, or expensive, intimidating, fancy design stores. Shabby Chic filled a void in the market for curated and gathered collections of well-made, tasteful furnishings for people with normal budgets who wanted something interesting but not too outrageous. Committing to Shabby Chic meant buying into a meaningful design movement with a clear philosophy and a soul.

Heaven's bedding: shades of white, lace, linen, and crystal create a lavish, romantic neutral palette.

Signature elements from the world of Shabby Chic:
elegant and timeless, with quiet, whispered details.

the shabby chic signature

On first impression, a Shabby Chic interior is one of unintimidating comfort, tattered elegance, romantic lighting, fresh flowers, and chandeliers. But underpinning this vision is a well-considered layer of practical detail, like dimmer switches, reading lamps, and washable covers, because function is just as important. I think the interior of a home should be a subtle experience, a feeling as much as a visual impact—just as a breathtakingly beautiful person can walk in a room and cause a fleeting moment of wow, but a person with character and soul leaves us wanting more. This lingering, calming, soulful effect is the one the Shabby Chic movement has had on people.

An oversize Shabby Chic Bloomsbury sectional sofa,
inviting for family gatherings. Washable slipcovers
add to the user-friendliness of Shabby Chic.

vintage flea market finds

Searching for vintage finds at flea markets has been the source magic and inspiration for me as long as I can remember. Finding threadbare fabrics and timeworn treasures is as exciting to me today as it ever was: in a moment I connect with the soul and history of items, and the patina, color, and texture that are evidence of love and life. Owning a piece of these beauties feels like a privilege I feel lucky to have discovered.

Vintage workbenches are one of my favorite finds. I love the chunky proportions and the layers of paint showing evidence of years of projects. Useful for kitchen islands or console tables, if space allows.

Tea time (made in a vintage tea pot) is a daily ritual for me.
However informal my tea time may be, I love the formality of using pretty
china, the more eclectic the better. My love for vintage china and glassware
is all encompassing: as dishwashing is not advised, I happily enjoy the daily
practice of hand washing, and truly appreciate my treasures.

My best piece of flea market advice: Go home empty-handed rather than with the wrong thing. It's perfectly okay to leave with nothing. As with many things in life, if you go with an organized mind, knowing what you are looking for, you will have the best chance of finding what you need. Consider what you already have, look at the piece on sale in the context of your home, then ask yourself: Is it beautiful? Is it comfortable? Is it functional?

On the practical side: Go prepared with a shopping list, a tape measure, and transportation to bring treasures home. As silly as it sounds, a flashlight has been a savior for me to make sure I was buying "on palette." Always take notes if you don't pick up your treasures as you go, and even write down the phone numbers of the vendors, as nothing is worse than finding a treasure and then losing it.

Flea markets are how I decorate my home and are at the core of the world of Shabby Chic. The beauty of treasure hunting lies in finding substantial little pieces, sometimes quite affordably, but treasures nonetheless...It's a way of acquiring interesting and individual items, with the quality and workmanship of days gone by. There is much redundancy in products in stores today. So much furniture is made overseas in huge quantities at more affordable prices than domestically, that finding high-quality pieces can be difficult as well as hugely expensive. While flea market finds might require a little, or sometimes a lot of, restoring before they can be reused and reloved, it can be well worth the trade-off, as proper dowel and screw joints will always make for a feeling of substance over glue, nails, and staples.

The flea market process in itself is enjoyable: the search, the find, the conversations, the stories of provenance—even if the truth is stretched—it's a chance for interaction with human beings, which is a value in itself. While there are some very good and attractive reproduction vendors at flea markets and antique shows, it's important you know what you are buying. Authentic vintage will likely always be a better investment to resell, and there is value in having something that is unique.

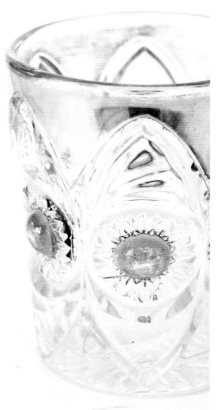

The glamour and bling of dinnerware comes from Shabby Chic touches of gold or lusterware.

CLOCKWISE FROM TOP LEFT: *A French creamer with brightly colored hand-painted flowers and gold-leaf scrolls and squiggles. Chunky glass with hand-painted gold and raspberry swirls. Fine white china with delicate gold floral decals. Petite fine glass vase with raised gold handwork.*

ABOVE: *A pink, swirly, lusterware plate.*

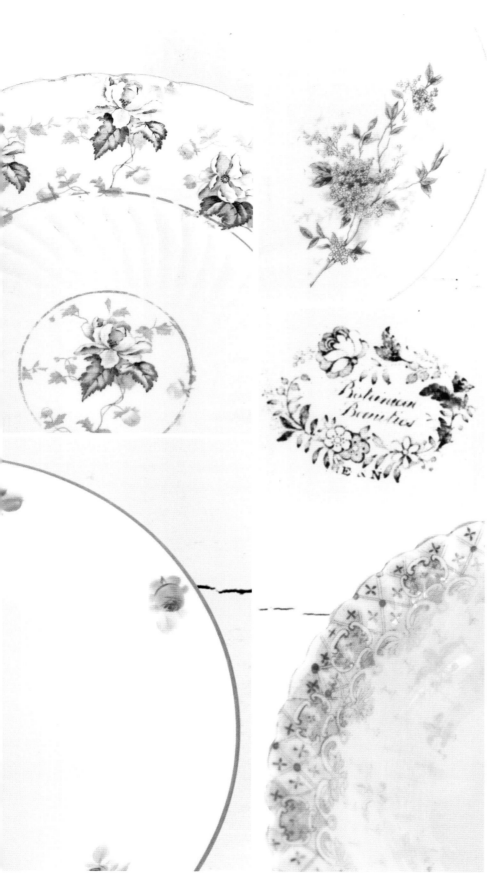

Along with mixing and matching colors and prints, I love to mix different techniques and styles of decoration.

CLOCKWISE FROM TOP LEFT: *Formal, orderly purple flowers around the rim of a desert plate. "Give us this day our daily bread" plate with hand-painted roses. Repeat pattern of turquoise irises with faded accents of gold. Ditsy flowers over a raised design. A favorite back stamp that gave inspiration for the Simply Shabby Chic logo. Faded fleur de lis turquoise and gold sugar bowl. Hand-painted pink and brown floral desert plate, one of my favorite color combinations. Simple purple geometric edging design. A favorite plate with cascading turquoise and green flowers. Decorative floral design with gold accent decal.*

Chandeliers and sconces are part of the Shabby Chic story.
While often thought appropriate only in fancy settings,
I like layering in the chic with the shabby.

CLOCKWISE FROM LEFT: *A vintage candlestick lamp of twisted glass*
sitting on a perfectly dulled silver base; the lace shade is a subtle extra;
I happily leave the flame-tip lightbulb without a shade. A gold frame
sconce, with pink tasseled shade, bedecked in crystals.

ABOVE: *A colorful bohemian chandelier may be unexpected in the*
world of Shabby Chic, but there are moments for a nice pause of color.
Simple and beautiful, this sconce is perfect for the mansion or the shack.

Florentine furniture and accessories are treasures I love to find. Originating from Italy, it's the Shabby way of adding over-the-top Renaissance-style elegance. A little nightstand, stationery box, bookends, a tissue-box, or magazine rack are gilded treasures. The European flair sits comfortably in the Shabby world of white, or in a soft, smoky-colored palette.

Vintage furniture is always such a pleasure to find—it speaks so perfectly to "beauty and function" in unique ways, as often the patina, palette, and quality of workmanship is impossible to find in today's world.

LEFT: *Shabby Chic details: Line the drawers of flea market treasures with wallpaper (vintage, if possible).*

CLOCKWISE FROM TOP LEFT: *A simple, slightly distressed white dresser made special with porcelain knobs and a scalloped skirt.*

Distressed pale green drop-leaf kitchen table and a couple of stools—all three pieces are wonderfully practical for a small space—dropping the leaves and scattering the stools means little space is needed day to day. (I come across many more kitchen tables than I do coffee tables. From time to time I will chop down the legs to about fifteen inches to transform a kitchen table into a coffee table.)

Pale, faded blue cabinet with a little distress and easy proportions make this a very sought-after piece as it is easy to fit in a home and hugely practical; it would bring an accent of unique character into a home with built-ins.

A touch of flaky turquoise paint is a welcome bright moment; the table is primitive in style but dainty of proportion, with its tapered legs.

A washed-out turquoise dresser, beachy in feel, the fancy scalloped skirt balances nicely with the backboard on the top; three deep drawers and casters for easy moving make this piece as beautiful as it is practical.

A rare pink kitchen table, probably once upon a time an extension table that lost its leaf along the way, is now fixed; chunky legs and much distress make this a perfect vision in my eyes.

All in pink. A primitive pie cupboard, a romantic French coffee table, and a pretty little end table, all very different in style but sitting together comfortably, joined by the common thread of pink. The mesh on the doors of the pie cupboard is a nice change from glass and the chipped painted knob on the little end table brings wonderful life to this piece. Gentle carving on the leggy low table is romantic but not over the top.

A symphony of vintage fabrics makes a masterpiece of a setting for any fancy event. I used layers of vintage lace curtains in a non-creamy ivory and scooped and swagged by layering in solid Belgian linen panels and two glorious lace and cotton runners with hidden pale blue silk bows. The draping and rumples are another example of the beauty of imperfection.

poplins, velvets, and treasured textiles

When I was first compiling my Shabby Chic collection of fabrics, I wanted to offer my customers an edited selection: denims, stripes, floral chintzes, solid colors, floppy velvets, and damasks—a whole range, but curated so the process of choosing wouldn't be overwhelming. I wanted the practical aspect of being able to pop everything in the washing machine; on the aesthetic side, I wanted the intimidating shiny newness erased. Back in the 1980s there was nothing like that on the market, so I started experimenting.

The washing part was interesting. There is an art and a science to this process, as the temperature of the water and the dryer, along with the type of soap and softener, all have to be considered. There is a well-known fabric store in Los Angeles, called Diamond Foam and Fabric, where you can buy fabric by the yard or in bolts of sixty yards. The owner, Jason, and I built up a rapport and I'd buy a yard of velvet, mattress ticking or damask to experiment with in the washing machine. If you put velvet in the wash, it goes all floppy; damask puckers beautifully; and denim shrinks. In this way, I learned my science and discovered formulas for what it took to create the perfect floppiness or the perfect puckeredness, the percentages of shrinkage, and the perfect degree of fade.

Remembering my mum's formula for the fabric she used in her antique-doll restorations, I experimented with tea-staining fabric to break down that pristine sheen and give an illusion of age. I started putting ten yards at a time in my kitchen sink with tea bags, but then I got to working with several little dye houses around town and we came up with a process that worked, but was tricky; although these processes are a science, they are also an art, and art is difficult to exactly duplicate from one batch to the next. Even Jason thought I was nuts, but for a minute back then, I monopolized the market with my washing and drying techniques, which varied from fabric to fabric.

In time, Shabby Chic had, alongside the ever-popular white-denim machine-washable slipcovers, a unique library of prewashed, preshrunk, enzyme washed, overdyed fabrics that looked gorgeous. Our main fabric sales are largely white and earth tones, linens and denims, but the florals, stripes, damasks, and bolder offerings are a crucial part of the range. Along with my own floral designs, I have always loved Bennison Fabrics, a UK-based company with the most gorgeous patterns and colors. I use sparingly as it's expensive, but it's worth every little yard.

To this day, white denim is our number one fabric. We lose about 20 percent in the washing and drying process due to shrinkage, but it's an affordable fabric and a gateway to the "wow" of white. Before Shabby Chic, the process of machine-washed upholstery fabrics, along with the aesthetic, had not yet been introduced to the marketplace. Home furnishing was much more tailored and uptight until my Shabby came along. Now if you go to fabric stores, it's commonplace to see swatches of prewashed fabrics. For proof of the Shabby Chic influence look no further than the Encyclopedia Britannica, where it states that in the 1990s, Shabby Chic was the most innovative design movement in the home furnishing market. (A proud moment for me!)

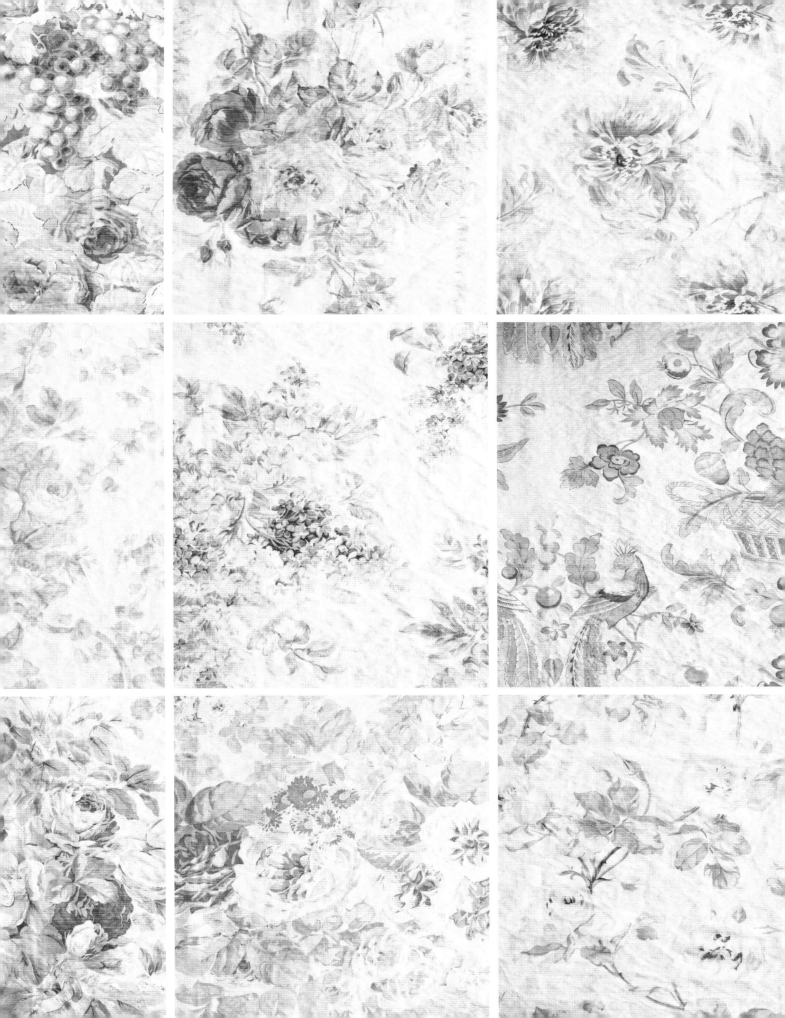

PREVIOUS PAGE, LEFT: *Bolts of washed-out and faded Shabby Chic fabrics.*
PREVIOUS PAGE, RIGHT: *A patchwork of my favorite muted Bennison fabrics. The palette and exquisite shading of flowers is unmatched by any other fabric line. They still silk-screen by hand to control the subtle brilliance of the patterns.*

Floral fabrics are synonymous with the world of Shabby Chic.
ABOVE: *Wildflower Floral Pink was one of my first designs and set my journey into fabric design.* RIGHT: *I usually use poplin for my bedding and a soft washed linen for my furniture. In both cases I like to create a sense of faded, washed beauty that still feels fresh and crisp.*

While Shabby Chic will always be famous for our white and ivory slipcovers, it is a nice option to change covers for the seasons: a petite pink floral print is the perfect accent for the summer months.

Freshly cut roses from my garden. Each stage, from bud to blossom to falling petals, brings me joy.

fabulous flowers

Flowers are the soul of my aesthetic and design work. They are a constant source of inspiration for their color, abundance, and simplicity. The cycle of life of flowers and nature is a constant reminder to me to embrace the imperfect, to celebrate newness, however fleeting, and to accept the inevitable. For me, every stage of a flower's life has its beauty, from the first little bud to the blossom and falling petals. I celebrate each stage, often with different vases that compliment the process, from a bud vase to a large vintage vase and ending with some petals in a discarded saucer.

A vase of fresh-cut flowers, however small, shows recent attention and love—a virtually empty room will not feel abandoned if there are flowers. The process of preparing fresh-cut flowers is a Zen moment for me.

I am blessed with a glorious garden that blossoms most of the year, due to that California climate, but when I am not home and in need of flowers, I am pleased that these days flowers are so easy to find. My favorite place to buy them is a flower market, but corner stores and supermarkets are good options, too. I am not ashamed of filling in the voids with fake flowers and I have tricked many with my collection of fabric roses, peonies, larkspur, delphiniums, and wisteria. My garden, and working with flowers, gives me endless joy, inspiration, and peace.

LEFT: *A selection of English roses from the renowned rose breeder*
David Austin, displayed in vintage vases, often pieces that have lost their lids.
I tend to discard most of the stems and greenery and just focus on the blooms.

ABOVE, CLOCKWISE FROM TOP LEFT: *Leftover buds of roses, stocks,*
and lisianthus for the birdbath. The floral tower is a work in progress
made mainly of fake delphiniums and roses—so realistic and a gorgeous
"forever-to-keep" piece. Walking on my garden path.

LEFT: *Glorious lilacs.*
ABOVE: *In my element; just back from the flower market and in my garden prepping flowers.*

Hand-painted documented illustrations are often the starting point for my fabric designs. Sometimes I change the scale, sometimes the color, but it is easier for me than starting with a blank canvas.

BUILD a Little Fence of Trust,
    Just around to-day;
Fill the space with Loving deeds,
    And therein stay,
Look not through the sheltering bars
    Upon to-morrow,
God will help thee bear
    Whatever comes, of Joy or Sorrow.

Flowers find their way into so many details in the world of Shabby Chic.

Happiness
is a perfume
you cannot pour
on others without
getting a few drops
yourself

CLOCKWISE FROM LEFT: *Floral watercolor art often prettifies a profound poem or saying. Painted flowers on a metal canister, probably Italian. Porcelain flowers applied to a brass candlestick; some have chips that I may camouflage with a blob of nail polish, but it's still so beautiful in its imperfectness. Vintage silk and velvet flowers are hard to find these days, but when found, a quick steam over the kettle brings back their shape and bounce. A treat of a plate—hand-painted flowers on lusterware—lovely for holding a candle, soap, or even boring paperclips.*

pretty floral prints

In the world of Shabby Chic, floral prints are part of the core signature. There is something so nostalgic and classic about floral prints, and the more that mix and match together, the better. Fading from the wash or the sun is, in my world, a valuable asset. I get excited at what treasures I may find at textile shows or among the piles of fabrics at the flea market and what these precious pieces may aspire to become. Vintage fabrics are nearly always the starting point for my collections. Sometimes I change the palette, sometimes the scale, but the vintage base is where I like to start. I am very particular about the types and designs of flowers in my prints. I am drawn to ditsy roses and big cabbage roses; I love fine handwork, as well as a looser, more watercolor approach, but I avoid anything that feels kitschy or too defined.

Floral paintings, floral designs on threadbare needlepoint rugs, and floral handwork or decals on china tea sets are all signature elements of Shabby Chic, and are typically faded, barely there, crackled, and wonky—but the imperfection needs to be perfect; that combination makes for a visual symphony.

Drying fabrics on washing lines brings me joy; it's a common sight in my garden and at The Prairie—as it was at my mum's and now my daughter's. With the Californian sun, fabric fades easily (of course this wasn't an issue with washing lines in London) and in my design work I've tried to replicate this effect with distressed screens that break down crispness when printing a floral fabric. There are so many interesting washes, stone washes, and enzymes, as well as garment-dying techniques that it can be hard to tell what's authentic from what's been recently treated to look that way. It is a challenge to work with these treatments for home furnishings, as we usually need much larger amounts of fabric to make our products than the clothing industry, and it's sometimes tricky to find vessels big enough to handle large quantities, but whatever way they are produced, sun-bleached, washed-out florals are a Shabby Chic staple.

PREVIOUS PAGE: *An archive of years of Shabby Chic bedding prints.*

ABOVE: *While white bedding and upholstery is the core of Shabby Chic, floral bedding is also part of our signature. I am very specific in my design work: roses and other florals have to have the depth of detail that feel authentic to prints of days gone by. And the palettes of pinks, blues, and greens is very specific. This is a sampling of some of our all-time favorites.*

the wow of white

My love affair with white came from two places. The first was a real appreciation of the light and openness of California, even though my English soul feels most comfortable on gray dreary days. The second is that white is a reflection of my basically shy personality. Even though I have always had a strong point of view, it took me years to find my voice. White was my way of creating a bold wow factor without shouting too loudly or putting a stake in the ground with an opinion. White is a neutral wow. My first big success was the white-denim slipcovers that, wash after wash, come up lovely and new. I will forever be indebted to white, and I will forever live in white.

Texture plays an important role in the commitment to a white interior. Plain white walls can be subtly enhanced by adding a chair rail with painted anaglypta paper below, or by a molding around the ceiling or lace curtains; these are all are options I have used in my own home and in design projects to bring depth to white. White can take on so many different feelings: lace and linens contribute a lovely breezy feel, white silk taffeta is icy and elegant, and a heavyweight white fabric with white furry throws can bring substance to a winter wonderland.

Then there's the tricky issue of which white is right. There are many shades of white to choose from. Personally, I avoid creamy yellow whites, gray hues, or anything too stark and bright. It is wise to do a paint test in situ because you never know how light falling on a wall will affect the result.

I often get asked what white paints I use. These are my favorites: Sherwin-Williams *Ultra White*, Valspar *Extra White*, Gliden *Brite White*, Farrow & Ball *All White*, and Farrow & Ball *Wombourne*, for a moodier white.

PREVIOUS PAGE: *Heavenly white tablecloth and transparent accessories. Peaceful and calming. An "ahhh" moment.*

ABOVE: *A white petticoat tablecloth cascades onto the cement floor. Raw elegance.*

RIGHT: *Our beloved Darcy chair, named after the dashing Mr. Darcy from* Pride and Prejudice, *in recognition of the forever romance of this chair.*

A bird's-eye view of the beauty of vintage white dinnerware—mainly Limoges and other French one-of-a-kind treasures. The hodgepodge of styles breaks down the intimidating feeling that a perfect, matching white table might create. White roses and other bits and bobs add playfulness and, in my mind, create a symphony.

LEFT: *A Shabby Chic sitting room—sometimes it's nice to be a grown-up and to be proper, while still honoring beauty, comfort, and function.*

ABOVE: *Shabby Chic signature white ruffles.*

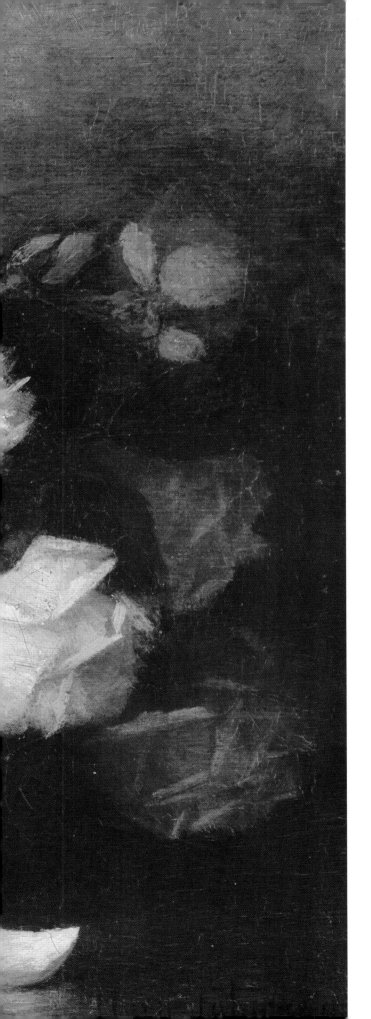

the shabby palette

It has evolved. In my first book it was about white and white. But since then, additions to my palette of soft pinks, grays, and blues are the result of my growing confidence. I have bleached wood floors in my home, and I appreciate varying shades of (non-orangey) woods both on floors and in furniture, whereas before I'd have painted everything white. Now my pinks have scaled into raspberry, and the pastels have taken on smokier tones. No-no colors for me are still black, gem tones, terracotta and creamy yellow white—and red and green: Christmas in my home is pink and silver set in a white wonderland.

I like to bring in little pops of color, either with painted flea market pieces, vintage wallpapers or reclaimed floor tiles. Less is more with these elements, both for effect and for the budget. With so much shopping online now, I have to be mindful about how my designs will translate digitally. We have a "Barely There"' print, that, online, is not there at all, so I've had to learn to tell my story in an online way. Although my palette's getting stronger, I will always be on the whiter shade of pale.

My color inspiration comes from many sources: movies, magazines, and particularly ballet and dance, with all its different shades of pink and the choice of laces, silks, and velvet used in sets and costumes. Nail polish is also mesmerizing to me—there seems to be an infinite number of shades of pink, lavender and blue out there, and I often buy extra bottles to add to my library of inspiration.

My mood boards are an important part of how I process my stories and vision; they are often a work in progress for many weeks. I add and take away ideas as they either settle into place or fall out of the story. Today there is so much visual information via the Internet that it can be bewildering and addictive, but I do enjoy sharing my process of design and inspiration via Pinterest and Instagram—it's a valuable community where, as a designer, you can gauge interest before you go too far down the creative road.

There is a preconceived idea of the Shabby Chic aesthetic. Over the years, pink flowers and flaky white paint have decorated many little girls' bedrooms worldwide. I am proud to have become so identified with prettiness, but I also have been evolving my palette so it can sit as well in the master bedroom and in gender-neutral living rooms. Scaling my pastel palette into a smokier one has supported this evolution beautifully. A dove gray linen and sovereign gray velvet have become mainstays among our popular fabrics, side by side with our signature whites.

PREVIOUS PAGE: *Pink rose painting that is perfection to me—the pinks offset against the darker and smokier palette of the background. This has given me many years of inspiration in my design work, and is one of my top ten "forever-to-keep" pieces.*

ABOVE: *A pink sketch for an interior that I often refer to for shading of pink inspiration.*

ABOVE: *A Marie Antoinette chair with smoky pink upholstery on a fancy gold carved chair.*

RIGHT: *Pink and silver are my Christmas colors (no green or red). This little Santa is a signature Shabby Chic ornament. A tiny, pleated, pink ruffle and an overscale floral print demonstrates the small and specific range of the Shabby Chic pink palette. Pink paint on carving: this is the sugary pink that I often refer to. Farrow & Ball Middleton Pink is an all-time favorite.*

Blue inspiration.

ABOVE: *I keep the sailboat painting (with its little touch of pink) close by to refer to the blue and teal when I work with this palette.* RIGHT: *Tulle ruffles and silk ribbons are glorious to me, revealing shades of color and texture.* FOLLOWING PAGE: *Twenty shades of blue. I love blue and pink equally, although there is wider palette of blue that I love, from faded pastel blue to smoky gray, rich teal, and bright turquoise and aqua.*

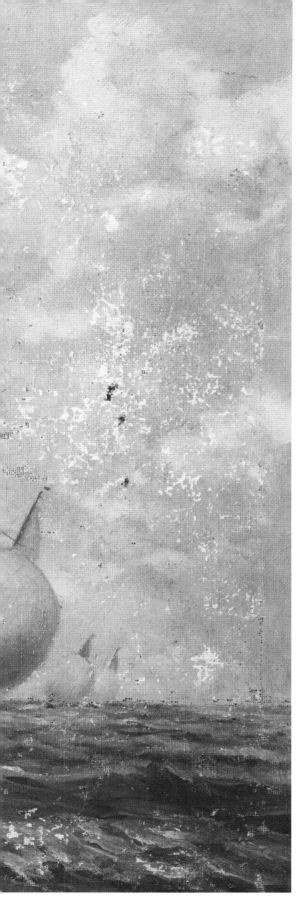

Purple fashion. I would only use as small accent moments, but I recognize its powerful beauty.

CLOCKWISE FROM TOP: *Vibrant colors from a painting of the desert; the palette reflecting exactly in my Shabby world. Lilac roses cascade down a slightly off-palette Majolica appliqué vase. A froth of zingy turquoise and purple tulle.*

RIGHT: *Not to be ignored: Shabby's Portobello chair-and-a-half in a squashy washable purple velvet.*

Magical patina needs years to develop, by way of chipped paint, cracks, woodworm trails, and bumps and scratches.

the shabby patina

Old, worn, shabby, tactile, crumbly pieces that wear their patina as history make for visual poetry, and in their wonky, worn, or fragile state, they still have a strength and poise. Texas is my source for weathered patinas and it's why, for many years now, my loyalty lies in the markets of Round Top, outside Austin. I can always count on finding lovely, simply built cabinets, tables, and dressers, old and worn, charming and soulful, with multiple layers of paint showing through because paint flakes off easily in the harsh Texas sun, and nobody bothers to strip and sand and start again, they just put on another layer.

Patina is such an important element in all period furniture no matter its origins, humble or grand. *Downton Abbey*, for instance, has caused quite the stir on both sides of the Atlantic as it seems everbody wants a bit of aristocratic, glamorous chic. There's a particular pink sofa in the family drawing room of Downton Abbey that is a quintessential period piece and seems to generate a lot of excitement. It is certainly a beautifully art-directed show, although I would love to add some evidence of the dramatic lives lived—by way of some mushy cushions, some rumpled beds, a bit of patina.

CLOCKWISE FROM LEFT: *An authentic distressed white and blue cabinet, rich in its imperfection. A reclaimed wood wall and corrugated ceiling make a handsome backdrop for shabby flowers. A darker wood patina with white blotches is a nice counterbalance to distressed white paint. An ornately carved pink arch from a visit to colorful India. The rich patina of distressed teal paint on a simple chest of drawers. Hand-painted Italian flowers, scraped and faded to a tattered elegance. Mellow brass fancy hardware, a treasure on a treasure. A cement birdbath; just enough remains of white and turquoise paint to still be pretty. Blue floral decals on white painted metal; a rusty patina bleeds through for extra authentic patina.*

LEFT: *An example of Shabby white-gray patina. Woodworm holes, barely there white-gray paint, a teeny drop of aqua,and plenty of irregular cracks and rusty patches speak of a life well-lived.*

ABOVE, CLOCKWISE FROM TOP LEFT: *Appliqués on a column, clogged up by years of over painting, are less precious but still romantic. Painted purple flowers (gypsy style) on an ivory cabinet from Hungary. A fine French carved leg in shabby white paint. White paint, hardware, and a keyhole—basics from the Shabby Chic world. A quintessential Shabby ivory paint, original roses and swags with glass protecting the flaky paint top.*

A New Moon cupboard displaying its humble, patched-up origins;
it has the palest, faded pinkish white paint and a teeny hint of a green past.

LEFT: *The casually discarded dress tells a Shabby Chic story.*

layers of love and life

For me, life is about a gentle tweaking—letting certain things go and layering in new treasures rather than clearing the decks and starting over. My design work, in a way, is a metaphor for my values in life. Life is about a series of adjustments; it's fluid, circumstances change, we evolve. Rarely is there a need to let everything go, we can simply adjust.

My style is defined by a room that feels evolved and fluid, as opposed to designed and delivered. My furniture collections are created to last a lifetime. Slipcovers and cushions may change over time, but I enjoy the idea that the bones of my designs and products endure along with memories that are saved. When I place pieces in a home, whether for myself or for a client, it is with great consideration and appreciation for how they fit in the space. My work is not about fads, but about quality, history, and soul. It's a rare day that I would feel the need to change out a whole room—perhaps an accent pillow, or maybe a throw to refresh. Much of my bedding collections mix and match and layer together, which creates another opportunity to bring in newness without discarding the old.

I use my flea market finds as accent pieces to bring old and new together, and to create a soulful, welcoming feeling. It is with these accents—with the costars—that I get braver with my palette. I might pop in a bright turquoise dresser, not center stage but in the role of balance, and suddenly a broken-down dresser, coaxed along with some gentle restoration but still embracing its imperfection, is promoted from understudy to star.

PREVIOUS PAGE: *A smoky palette of pinks and teal lace,*
linen, and ruffles draped in organized chaos on the kitchen table.

ABOVE: *Linen and lace in washed-out shades of teal,*
pale pink, and lilac teach the perfect color lesson.

My aesthetic sits with what feels right rather than with a rule-book of "interior design." My own home is a carefully balanced, eclectic hodge podge, but it is uncluttered, with mindful placement of each treasure. There does need to be method to the madness. Mixing and matching takes a discerning eye to follow the flow and build an overriding feeling that is soft on the eye, individual and welcoming and, in the end, truly representative of the world of Shabby Chic.

I have a growing appreciation for modern clean lines and architecture, as I find a gentle humility in the simplicity. In the past I was a bit stuck with crumbly castle properties, which I do still love, but now I can also see myself in a modern simple space, knowing my signature pieces will bring comfort to the rooms. With the right choice of furnishings conveying soul and emotion, I see how a simple space can be a graceful platform to make a comfy home. A home should be a manifestation of how we live. For instance, I have one junk drawer in my kitchen, a messy dumping ground of confusion and uncertainly, but order reigns everywhere else. My home reflects me: it's my art. I avoid clutter—if you don't use it, then lose it—and aspire to purposefulness in each room. At the end of the day, what we all need is a home that mindfully reflects who we are as people.

*The business and I grew up together,
learning along the way to hold to a vision.
My mantra is to work hard and stay in my
passion and then the story finds its way.*

storytelling

I had a boyfriend who believed Shabby Chic was my biggest love affair—not because I was addicted to work, but because Shabby Chic received my heart, my soul, my love. My relationship with romance can be seen in my design work, in the music I listen to, and in the movies I connect with. They fuel me and I recycle my emotions back into Shabby Chic. My comfort with the incomplete, the imperfect, the quiet, and the faded is directly related to my emotional comfort, and I think this is what resonates with people when they touch and feel the world of Shabby Chic.

For many years I have honed my craft to curate and present Shabby Chic products in my stores so that my story translates to the customer in a way they can identify with. Some people know what they want and like to furnish their houses themselves, and simply need to see and be inspired in order to make their choices. At the other end of the scale, a customer may have a vision and an opinion, but need some help bringing the vision to life. When I've helped to design homes for others, I try to do so by asking questions and proposing solutions that empower the customers to find their own answers that my team or I can then execute. Anyone who relates to Shabby Chic would likely be someone who is gentle and looking for a nurturing home, so the more they can look inward to find their answers, the more their home will reflect them. Whenever I design anything, from a room to a label, little stories pop into my head: There's always that little sprinkle of soul in everything I touch.

3

the looks of shabby chic

The world of Shabby Chic evokes a romantic and feminine vision of flaky white paint, soft white ruffles, and pink flowers. That look will always hold a special place in my heart, but many other aesthetics, palettes, and patinas now belong in the visual vocabulary of Shabby Chic. Over the years it has diversified and evolved, while staying true to the core values of beauty, comfort and function.

R

ROMANTIC GLAMOUR

Jessica Simpson has had quite the career, from pioneering reality TV to singer and now heading up a vast licensing empire. Paparazzi follow her every move, which comes with the territory of being a celebrity these days; hence "home" is a sacred place of privacy.

Jessica had been a fan of Shabby Chic and when she was pregnant with her first baby, she contacted me to decorate the nursery; I was flattered that she requested I bring my Shabby world into her sanctuary. She and her husband Eric were very involved with the process. They had very specific ideas that I carefully considered. I created a mood board to show them ideas of palette and style. She has a public persona of beauty, romance, a gypsy streak, and a little bit of country, all of which I took into account as I pulled together a vision. I have a private collection of vintage wallpaper that I use for VIP projects. A pattern featuring butterflies together with a bohemian chandelier became the anchors of the nursery.

Little by little my small design team and I gathered beautiful, comfortable, and practical treasures for the nursery. As we were fast approaching completion, Jessica and Eric decided that before their baby was born, they wanted a touch of Shabby Chic throughout their home, so we quickly transformed the lovely bones of their house to a romantic love nest; in addition we decorated for a birthday party, which we held in her festive garden, flanked by huge trees that created a lot of shade, as well as privacy from prying paparazzi.

The house had a nice meandering feeling to it, although some areas lacked light, which I embraced by making them cozy. The house wasn't very large, and with visiting family members on both sides, I wondered how long it would be before they outgrew it.

Classic cushy slipcovered furniture, twinkly chandeliers, and an imperfect carved gold mirror give balance to Jessica's inviting but traditional living room. After baby Maxwell was born, this is where a group of us had weekly Weight Watchers meetings. Such meetings have never been so comfy.

PREVIOUS PAGE: *Formal romance in the master bedroom, and Bentley.*

A formal love seat upholstered in a classic Bennison fabric and set under a whimsical Chagall sketch is made inviting and comfortable with a hodgepodge of vintage decorative pillows.

My job was to bring a youthful, comfortable, and comfy feel to the classic interiors, keeping a traditional, but unstuffy look. The living room was hardly used because it was a bit stiff and unwelcoming—it needed an overhaul of both furniture and furnishings. I incorporated Bennison fabrics in soft, muted colors and hid some rather Las Vegas-type roman columns with an elegant, understated curtain. I gave her overstuffed chairs new slipcovers and cushions, and made some new comfy pieces all staged on a lavish, lovely rug from the Rug Company. Once complete, this room got a whole new lease on life.

The dining room has simple bones but transforms easily by layering in decadent furnishings complementing Jessica's family-loving feminine side, and balancing glamour and informality. The Farrow & Ball wallpaper is a moment of tradition; the chandelier, the mix-and-match china, and the religious icon moment are pure Shabby Chic.

The master bedroom portrays the way my blue palette has evolved from the earlier palest pale blue to a smokier teal with accents of a stronger blue. The room is classic, comfortable, and gorgeous. The bed is ginourmous and one that both Eric and Jessica had strong feelings about keeping—but it was black leather! So that got white denim slipcover, which transformed it into a cloud.

We went room by room through the house, making many extra sleeping spaces for family visitors who were to come out for the baby's birth. Beautiful baby Maxwell was born, and the nursery became the core of the house. A few short months later, and Jessica and Eric were expecting another baby along with the reality of "outgrowing the house." Jessica ended up buying Sharon Osbourne's house, featured in a prior book of mine—small world.

Shades of blue vintage chenille and linen fabrics made into a symphony of blue pillows.

CLOCKWISE FROM TOP LEFT: *Vintage china plates nestled into an abundance of ruffles. Perfectly dripping candles making a beautiful mess. The blue and white plates do not match but they complement one another.*

RIGHT: *Jessica and Eric's formal dining room is a little bit Marie Antoinette and a little bit traditional, adding up to complete romance. The subtle silvery wallpaper is Silvergate by Farrow & Ball, the Darcy chairs and Petticoat tablecloth are from Shabby Chic, and the vintage glassware and china are carefully curated. French tulips, lisianthus, and roses make for magic.*

Jessica and Eric's bedroom is their sanctuary and their nest. The room has a formal Marie Antoinette quality that promises total comfort and full-on romance with no unnecessary chaos. An oversize bed has been transformed with a white denim slipcover; the teal bedding is from Shabby's Petticoat Collection. Pale blue velvet gives a pair of Shabby white vintage formal chairs a new lease on life, an oversize carved mirror anchors the romance in the room, and teal velvet curtains bring a pop of drama into an otherwise soft palette.

ABOVE, CLOCKWISE FROM LEFT: *Shabby ruffle details and a pop of brilliant turquoise from a precious fleamarket colored glass.*

RIGHT: *Eric has a corner in the ruffled princess paradise. The chunky primitive desk and leather-upholstered vintage Time-Life office chair are a place for Eric to write and for Jessica's girlie bits and bobs – a rickety blue decorative birdcage and a wallpapered barrel – to blend beautifully and practically.*

Frilly frou-frou curtains and a chandelier over a freestanding tub set the stage for decadence.

Jessica's beautification nook. It's small but includes all that is needed to transform Jessica from a truly natural beauty into a glamorous star. The simple palette of silver gilt and pale blue is quietly glamorous.

The guest room is theatrical and glamorous, with Farrow & Ball gold and cream medallion wallpaper, a pale blue tufted headboard, and vintage bits and bobs.

Faded denim blue accents in the guest room.
The naked lampshade allows the marble
bust lady to take center stage with just a
vintage silk flower for decoration.

Jessica's garden playground. The little vintage playhouse and playful prom dresses make for fantasy time. I like to take flowers into the house and decorate the garden with fabrics and ribbons, exchanging visual delights.

ROMANTIC GLAMOUR
PORTFOLIO

The two architectural styles that people most associate with Shabby Chic are the cottage and romantic traditional, which inevitably bring with them a life history and a patina of time-worn qualities. Paneling, moldings, and tile work usually come with the territory, making a lovely stage and platform to layer in signature Shabby Chic elements of vintage furniture, chandeliers, and threadbare or faded rugs. The challenge faced in many period homes is that often they can be overly busy to the eye. I like a quiet background, but I will always protect and honor authentic details, even if decadent and grand. White paint works well as a neutralizer, allowing the charm of details to quietly take center stage. Observing how the light plays and moves in a house is valuable before too many decorative decisions are made and learning where shadows fall alters color.

Traditional doesn't need to be stuffy; it makes a good marriage with Shabby Chic informal florals, a mix-and-match approach to furniture—no uptight matchy-matchy—and Shabby Chic's signature eclectic, soft, and inviting ambiance with generous displays of floppy garden flowers that help deflect any inherited formality. And unexpected moments help add accents of surprise: I love adding pauses of wallpaper in typically uncalled for places, and I'm a great lover of nooks and always give them a decorative acknowledgment as even though they aren't real rooms, they are often cherished spaces..

Seems to me, most of us live less formally in our homes today, despite our love affair with *Downton Abbey*. My mantra is "if you don't use it, lose it," and that goes for formal dining rooms and living rooms, replaced now with the communal spaces of open plan kitchens and family rooms. When Shabby Chic gets layered into a traditional home, it embraces the classic, adds some frou-frou, loosens it up, and makes every corner livable and welcoming.

CLOCKWISE FROM LEFT: *Romance continues. A perfectly pretty ensemble featuring a charcoal ballet sketch, floppy pink roses, and a delicate 1950s cabinet. The quiet magic of a metal arch of flowers. Life imitates art, art imitates life— pink tole tray from Italy with David Austin English roses.*

Shabby Chic tradition with a twist. A mahogany bed, painted white to bring it into the world of Shabby Chic, and abundant, romantic, fluffy bedding complements the eclectic vintage cabinets, a gold settee, a pastel rose painting, and a signature Lily Juliana chandelier. The modern setting of a raw cement wall and modern metal window frame is a nice juxtaposition.

PREVIOUS PAGE: *Traditional palette and patina in the world of Shabby Chic,* FROM LEFT TO RIGHT: *A vintage cotton lace curtain with cotton stitching. A ruffled shade and a beautifully imperfect silk flower. Delicate gilded details on glass.*

NEXT PAGE: *A rainbow of imperfectly garment-dyed smoky velvet ruched pillows.*

SHABBY SPANISH

Spanish style is typically a little too rich for me, with its signature raw terracotta palette and festive colors, but I do love the way Spanish architecture meanders organically through courtyards, balconies, and archways. I relate to the off-centeredness. The house shown here is owned by Lisa Henson and her husband David—Lisa is the daughter of the late Jim Henson of Muppet fame—who I met through mutual friends. From the moment I entered the property, I saw a beautiful blending of Shabby Chic and the Spanish style. I had no role in decorating this house but had much appreciation of its beauty and was inspired.

The outside spaces have a comfortable elegance, with a silvery light palette of olive trees and light stonework, with archways promising cool shade around the pool. The dining room looks onto a courtyard offering cross breezes and cross light. The deep red carpet is a little off my palette, but it is tempered, as most of the colors in the room are threadbare, faded, and quite lovely, but elegantly anchored with a truly spectacular crystal chandelier.

I like the idea and tradition of a reading room. Beautifully placed in this home but sadly a rare need today with the invention of electronic reading devices. The guest room is my favorite room in the house; I love the whimsically painted floor and the dark bed. There is a perfect balance of a warm and appealing room that is not over-personalized, so it is welcoming to all guests. The hallway serves as memory lane, with a picture wall of growing up with the Muppets, an experience rich in humor, love, and fun—a spirit that pervades every quirky corner of this home.

PREVIOUS PAGE: *Gathering my flowers and fabrics to prepare for the photo shoot at Lisa and David's house, which was designed by interior decorator Madeline Stuart. The very Spanish entrance is simple but delightfully decorative, teasing the eye for what lies beyond, which is an untypically faded Spanish palette that I just love.*

LEFT AND ABOVE: *The dining room is a Spanish mellow drama with a faded red rug and a shimmer of pale silk curtains. Chandeliers are a complete Shabby Chic signature—this one is made of rock crystal and is really chunky. It's lovely juxtaposition of twinkle and heft.*

Colorful Capo-di-Monte pieces are whimsical storytellers. These are just cheap market finds, but chosen very carefully. Some pieces can be quite crudely modeled, but these are beautiful and the petal detail is very fine.

Saturated Shabby Chic colors: an Ushak rug, an Indonesian table, and eclectic Shabby china and glass. This is the colorful end of the Shabby Chic palette.

LEFT: *Formal whimsy in the library is achieved with the overscale paisley chairs. A reading room of the past, well loved and utilized in this home.*

Hallways and nooks that you walk past every day get attention and make a good place for family memories. Here Jim Henson, Kermit the Frog, and other legends sit with Lisa and David's family history.

An invitation to cool, breezy living. The guest room is gender neutral and not too personal. There are no prints or paintings on the cool blue walls and no busy rugs on the painted stenciled floor. Moroccan lamps and a floaty dress create a nice balance with the ethereal lace lampshades and Victorian linen top sheet on the bed.

I love the silvery glimmer of the olive trees and the pale stone surround of this pool, positioned near the house so passing breezes are cooled before they waft in through the colonnades—a useful tip from the Ancient Romans. The landscaping and courtyard are the work of garden designer Eric Solberg.

An array of hydrangeas, wax flowers, roses, and delphiniums are on their way to be placed around the house.

Modest beauty. Matching pure white beds with beige embroidered flowers separated by magnolia blooms is just that. The dark mahogany wood chair is a lovely, rich addition with a Spanish flair.

SHABBY SPANISH
PORTFOLIO

I was unfamiliar with Spanish colonial style until I moved to California. Very popular in the early twentieth century, these solid homes come with age, tradition, and quality craftsmanship. Built with thick, solid walls, and archways deliberately positioned for shade and the play of light shafting in through cool-to-the touch tiled courtyards, these homes fit with the California climate. They feel to me like homes built for festivities, charming both small and large, with typical splashes of bright color and meandering layouts, nooks that that lead from one place to another, making even large houses feel cozy and inviting.

I love the way they resonate with specialness, the way they can be grand, but in a humble way, I love the play of light and shade, and I do love seeing the signature elements of Spanish architecture take on a lighter palette with pale stonework and tiles on the blonder side of terracotta. When you marry the faded Shabby palette with Spanish and a touch of Greece, with a froth of bougainvillea, it's just lovely.

A flamboyant Spanish gold and teal daybed drowned in the opulence of teal silk jacquard floppy-ruffle bedding. Scrumptious.

PREVIOUS PAGE, CLOCKWISE FROM LEFT: *A slightly battered little cabinet (another of my top-10 "forever-to-keep" pieces) with Spanish-y handwork topped with an explosion of white peonies. Hammered ornaments are typical of the Spanish Colonial style—lovely little bits of quiet Spanish bling. Crisp cream linen napkins with paper flower napkin rings.*

FROM LEFT TO RIGHT: *A rich hand-painted artwork panel on canvas.
A chunky crystal light pendant reflected in a frameless mirror. A gloriously ornamental votive
candle stand and a bit of sparkly tulle — a corner of a Spanish church meets Princess Prom.*

BEAUTIFUL BOHO

One of the qualities of Shabby Chic is that it lives well in small intimate settings such as cottages, beach houses, and shacks—although, and funnily enough, I have been asked a few times to make big mansions feel cozy and cottagey. Grand styles need grand spaces, but this tiny craftsman's cottage, built in the late 1920s, was ready to embrace the Shabby. This is my daughter Lily's house in Venice Beach, an area once rundown and for many years considered the "wrong" side of town: today it is bursting with artistic people and young families, alongside some of the original bohemian residents. Lily is not alone in her migration to Venice Beach, a number of kids who grew up in the beach-loving community of Malibu have stretched the umbilical cord rather than breaking it completely.

Lily discovered the property—the seller was an artist herself—and while there was quite the flutter of eager buyers, Lily's promise to carry on the legacy of creativity clinched the deal. Every square inch of this little home is well-utilized. Lily can often be found (with her beloved dog, Sadie, always close by), working in the back garden studio, keeping sacred the ink and watercolor drippings staining the walls with stories of the previous artist.

She has many creative interests, including music, sewing, art, and an attraction to stories of strong and spiritual characters. Many of my mother's passions have transmitted to Lily; her process of arranging her creative chaos is a clear sign of the engrained DNA. The legacy continues.

PREVIOUS PAGE: *A house inspired by Russian folk cottages and pulled together with leftovers. The simple, wonky cabinetry and the table and chairs were happy Shabby leftovers inherited from the previous owner. The painted Indian screen partitions the kitchen from the living room; the kitchen door opens to the garden. The chairs were refreshed with Anastasia fabric from the Shabby Chic fabric collection.*

ABOVE: *The street door opens into a small, pale blue living room filled with hand-me-downs including the oversize, mushy, pale pink linen sectional sofa, that much-coveted prize corner spot, and an eclectic mix of leftover bits and bobs. On the wall is a cherished photo of June and Johnny Cash. Everything is lit with a teeny-tiny modest-but-powerful center light fitting.*

Lily's creative and diverse cultural corner: The Buddha is from
my mum and the striking watercolor is by Kim McCarty.

Of course Lily was raised with Shabby Chic but she lives a more colorful palette than I. She painted the walls of her sitting room a pale aqua that's still soft, fresh, and beachy, but a much braver move than I would have made. I suggested an inspiration of design be taken from humble Russian folk houses, which are modest, simple, but with bravado in touches of color, and a little less precious than the quintessential Shabby Chic—qualities I find rather charming. No glamorous chandeliers quite fit, just little metal hanging lamps that are a surprise in scale and in keeping with the Russian folk inspiration. In the kitchen we splurged on a patch of reclaimed French vintage tiles, bringing in a bit of gorgeous color and patina. Industrial light fittings are layered in among the vintage knickknacks to complete the young boho story.

Lily is a graduate of the prestigous Central Saint Martin's School in London. She has used her studies and her legacy in the creative world and she's an artist and fashion designer, buying vintage clothes from markets that she then reworks—honoring the appreciation of silk ribbons, pieces of lace, and boxes of bits that subliminally left an imprint on her from her grandmother. Lily's vintage treasures also serve as inspiration for her original clothing collection, Lily Ashwell. Her curated library of pretty frocks and sundresses live in her tiny second bedroom alongside a moment of vintage wallpaper.

There is a cohesive charm to every room in this little home. A small-scale dining table and chairs supports the Shabby Chic ethos of congregating in the kitchen, and the overall palette and the patterns are quirky but harmonious, all pleasing to the eye. While the house is small, the view from each room is of the charming little garden. Roses, a trumpet tree, and other random groundcovers make for sweet eye candy from every window. Art, beauty, and culture are evident in every nook of this 1,000-square-foot home. It feels like a playground for a fresh spirit of magical creativity. The values of Shabby Chic coexist in this home without compromise to Lily and her personal style.

Lily's pretty bedroom bathed in romantic cross light from several sources. Vintage wallpaper is hard to find and hard to hang, but so worth it. The curtains are vintage florals, and the floor is cheap and cheerful painted plywood. Eclectic accents come from the leftovers sitting side by side: a painted Hungarian chest paired with a fanciful Italian dresser.

ABOVE: *The Bathroom is a teeny-tiny precious place, humble but hugely practical. We added a boho flea market mirror, folksy blue detail, and a new marble slab, but all else is as was.*

RIGHT: *This is floral folk. A hand-painted Spanish nightstand and old tin can vases are made beautiful with hydrangeas and roses. This nightstand matches the Spanish daybed from my house— a double dose would have been too matchy for me, so Lily got the leftover.*

LEFT: *The sewing room has Pearl Lowe lace curtains and a vintage wallpaper on one wall, giving a beautiful, luxurious accent to this functional and inspirational space. The room was on the sweet side, and Lily's style isn't particularly sweet, so the frayed rug contributes a grittier aesthetic.*

DAVID HAMILTON TWENTY FIVE YEARS OF AN ARTIST

PREVIOUS PAGE: *The artist's studio. I love a room at the end of the garden to make magic in. The past is present here in the flaking paint and dripping ink inherited from the previous artist/owner.*

ABOVE AND RIGHT: *Work-in–progress watercolors decorate the breezeblock walls. A lace curtain is an unexpected choice in a some- what scruffy workspace, but it's a perfect example of shabby and chic. The chair was my mum's. Her artsy spirit had opted for a red paisley slipcover when given the choice of any fabric. As an heirloom rather than a leftover, it fitted perfectly into Lily's boho world.*

Grapes of Wrath meets Coal Miner's Daughter...and a little Shabby Chic. The wonky window isn't about to fall apart; all exposed parts are protectively sealed.

Hammocks are a big part of the Shabby Chic world: a humble luxury, they find their way into myriad Shabby environments. Lily considers her garden as another room in her cottage, hence her addition of a pretty plastic and practical rug. Another Shabby garden signature that Lily wanted to include is the washing line or drying rack, as she prefers sunshine and breeze to the harsh effects of a dryer on her clothes. And it wouldn't be a Shabby garden without the protection of the Virgin Mary, and it wouldn't be Lily's garden without Sadie the dog. In California, of course, the garden is in use 365 days of the year, and for most of the time there is wonderful foliage, but when it's not a blooming time, I'm big into fake flowers, which are so much more convincing than they used to be. In winter the garden is brought to life with fake delphiniums and sunflowers, a drying rack of pretty frocks.

*A gypsy style Shabby Chic Capri
chandelier is colorfully eclectic.*

BEAUTIFUL BOHO
PORTFOLIO

I grew up in a kind of bohemian home, so I am drawn to the qualities of this style: an eclectic mix of ethnic, cultural, and informal that is soulful, artistic, and light in spirit. I relate to an evolved collection of furnishings—a genuine bohemian home can only come together with time and gypsy travels. Bohemian is nomadic, and even if the bones of the house are grounded and solid, a bohemian home will always have a feeling of impermanence, with the treasures within somehow suggesting mobility.

Its direct connection with Shabby Chic, potentially more than with any other aesthetic, is in the ethos and value of mixing and matching. A three-piece suite will never find a place in a bohemian home. While "boho" may be a trendy term used now, it's an authentic design of frugality with "heirloom" pieces sourced from flea markets and other treasure-hunting haunts. For this style to work, the owner/curator typically puts in some emotional and artistic flair to transform his or her found treasures into something of his or her own while embracing the integrity of the original. In such a home, for instance, a wonky white cabinet may be embellished with hand-painted flowers, a simple coffee table made special with a lovely personalized lace runner, and all the elements magically pulled together to tell the owner's own nomadic, meandering tale.

Nostalgic Shabby print of days gone by has a folksy flavor.

FOLLOWING PAGE: *A Bohemian rhapsody of color:* LEFT: *Cabbage roses on the their beautiful last legs complement the rich color of the raised floral blue vase.* RIGHT: *A chippy teal blue detail of a dresser, a beautiful example of Shabby's evolving palette.*

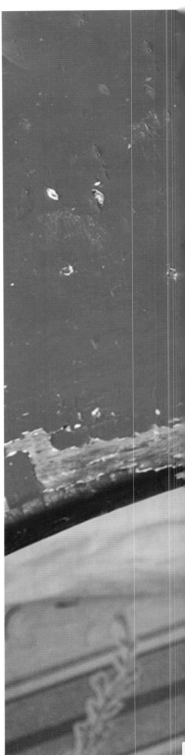

Three mismatched napkins all in a row, inspired by summer dress fabrics.

LEFT: *A mosquito net dyed pale pink drapes on a mattress that is simply plopped on the floor, boho hippy style. Florals on different scales add a pretty punch and take a bit of the sweetness out with their mismatchingness.*

ABOVE: *A naïve folksy flower design confidently carved into a pink wooden door.*

M

MAGICAL MODERN

When I first met Pamela Anderson back in the early 2000s, her personal taste was chandeliers and frills galore. I featured her quaint, crumbly, flaky cottage, quintessential to the Shabby aesthetic, in a prior book of mine, *Sumptuous Settings*. Changes in her tastes and needs gave her cause to demolish her Shabby cottage, which was just down the road from my Malibu home, so I observed the dismantling. She worked with the architect Philip Vertoch to manifest her vision to build a modern/Zen home on the same footprint. It took years to complete, due to planning problems, challenges with the building and her insistence on high-quality construction and detail.

The re-done house is beautifully made from teak, and it really is a labor of love. Sometimes modern homes can be trickier than any to build, as with the simple clean lines there is nowhere for imperfections to hide. After several years her home was complete, and while this modern home on its small cottagey footprint was a true masterpiece, Pamela felt it lacked some softness and sensual appeal.

PREVIOUS PAGE: *Pamela's living space is modern, elegant, and a little bit Zen. My job was to bring in a layer of comfy romance, so I focused on furnishing the space with mushy comfort, pure white slipcovers, warm woods, breezy linens, and beautiful flowers, while respecting the modern edges. Tropical cascading-cut orchids in the spare white fireplace vases are a gorgeous alternative to the usual Shabby roses and peonies.*

LEFT AND ABOVE: *A flaky painted table; heavy dark reclaimed wood on the cupboard doors, and the twinkle of a crystal chandelier softly complement the modern teak aesthetic.*

A subtle modern palette of grays and blues delivered in a signature Shabby fashion, by way of a green glass cross, a hydrangea bloom, and a lovely Bennison pillow.

It's hard to do messy in modern, but it can do comfort and mush, and I was able to bring the comfort and invitingness of Shabby Chic to a simple, minimalist interior. I used soft, white-linen-covered furniture, flowing linen gauze curtains to divide up the open plan spaces, flowers, of course, and a chandelier as a twinkle. In her previous home, Pamela's collection of beautiful books were displayed on open shelves in a chaotic but organized way, but the bookshelves did not translate and so we housed the entire collection in cabinets on either side of the fireplace behind heavy doors of reclaimed wood. The floaty, feminine painting of tutus over the fireplace actually has an edge to it, as it is built up from layers of plaster and has a cementlike texture. I kept a couple of signature Shabby pieces to join the dots of transition; a humble drop-leaf table sits sweetly on the simple stage.

Her media room is now a cloud of total comfort with wall-to-wall Shabby Chic overstuffed sofas, with no ruffles in sight, and on the walls sharp black-and-white photographs hold the modern line. Pamela likes the inviting and the mushy, but she likes a bit of formality, too, so amongst the comfy and breezy fabrics and furnishings, everything has a specific place. The canopy bed in the master bedroom is a quiet and simple frame for a gorgeous pile of comfort.

The kitchen is tiny, placed in the open plan living room, with modern open shelves, a polished concrete worktop, and sleek cabinets. We added the wooden beam for a bit of precise shabbiness. I think Pamela achieved her vision beautifully: a modern, Zen, spiritual home with plush, abundant luxury.

A wall-to-wall sofa moment in the media room that adjoins the living room and the kitchen. The family snuggle up here in a cloud of frill-free comfort and stripy duvets. The photos are by David Shuttlefield, the sofas are Shabby Chic white-linen sectionals.

Pamela's kitchen nook is on the far side of the stairs.
It is tiny, white, and very modern with handleless drawers
and a polished cement slab. We added the bleached wooden
beam. It's the perfect stage for flower arranging.

The master bedroom is sensual, serene, and beyond dreamy—
ruffles on ruffles and linen curtains dancing in the breeze.
It makes one big space with the bathroom. Truly heavenly.

ABOVE: *Tutu and flowers, barely there but beautiful.*
The painting is by French artist Laurence Amélie.

RIGHT: *Palette-perfect accessories curated*
around pretty boxes of chocolate truffles.

ABOVE: *Malibu holds a special place in my heart, as it does for Pamela. The inside/outside life feels so right. Sliding teak doors disappear into walls that lead to the pool area so indoor/outdoor boundaries blur. The pretty frock Pamela is wearing is one of Lily's.*

RIGHT: *Pamela's sky deck, where every square inch is well-utilized. We made the large teak daybeds and the turquoise and linen pillows. The oversize cushions are made of terry toweling, so it's practical bliss and still on palette. Pamela goes through frustrations with her teak decking as she hates orange, and teak has an orange tone every time it gets re-oiled, but it soon fades to beauty.*

FOLLOWING PAGE: *Cool and comfy, a teak hammock support, a simple crochet hammock, and an array of pillows and beachy cotton throws.*

MAGICAL MODERN
PORTFOLIO

"Modern" is a loosely used word that might not initially connect the dots to Shabby Chic. "Modern" to me means simple and streamlined design, uncluttered but rich in visual poetry. It has an undoubted appeal at certain stages of the life process, particularly at the empty-nest stage when kids' clutter is relegated to attics or basements, and a yearning sets in for a cleaner, simpler vista. I'm entering into this less-is-more stage myself. I've always believed that uncluttered closets mean an uncluttered mind, and while I embrace evidence of my life lived thus far by way of my children, art, and photo galleries on the walls, I find myself curating and editing many of my possessions. Shabby Modern is not an intimidating aesthetic, it's not severe or cold, it still has mushy cushions and floppy roses, but maybe also some floppy cut orchids, soft music, textured non-color, and spaces that inspire quiet and inward orientation.

Shabby Modern still embraces the beauty of imperfection, where life's knocks and dings are proudly evident and the simplicity of design reflects humility and modesty.

In my New York store we have an area called the "No Frill Zone," which is a showcase for the minimal manly moment. Our signature Soho bed is low and squishy, modern and upholstered; our big sectional sofas have beauty, comfort, and function in abundance. All encompassing the values of the Shabby Chic brand, but without a ruffle or a flower in sight.

PREVIOUS PAGE: *Faded stripes, and floppy linen, inviting and
frou-frou free. Total comfort contrasted with a rough concrete wall.*

ABOVE: *Chunky vintage furniture with straight lines;
beautiful unique industrial hardware; and just enough flaky paint—
classic Shabby, but fitting in perfectly with modern architecture
and elements, bringing an old soul to something new.*

A modern palette of white, gray, glass and smoky blue. A bit of bling and shimmer gives the hard edge of modern a friendly, Shabby moment.

ABOVE: *Floppy cut orchids cascade down a sculptural and sober white vase usually saved for drooping roses.*

RIGHT: *A bedding story of plains and restrained florals from the Shabby Chic bedding collection: Rose Bouquet Teal, a classic print with a fresh, modern vibe, mixed with White Whisper Belgian linen.*

A spare wooden four-poster: whimsy and romance
live beautifully together in a modern loft-like space.
It is always important to me to have enough accents in
a room to soften the edges and layer some romance,
by way of flowers, a chandelier or a soulful chair.

E

ECLECTIC ELEGANCE

I've lived in California for thirty-five years now, so even though nothing gives me more joy than a cozy English country cottage with rain dripping down the windows, I admit there's no more life-enhancing place to live than in the light of California. I have finally become quite attached to my home; my hat is hung! It is the first home I have owned as a single person. It's a nice balance between a house for me and my work, a place for the children to come visit, and an open house for friends and visitors. I do have a lot of sleepover guests, sometimes up to eight or ten, and beauty, comfort, and function reside in every room. The bones are a hodge-podge: from certain points of view it looks like an English house, from others like a Plantation house and the fireplace as though from a big Welsh manor—it happily accepts furnishings from all the diversities of Shabby Chic.

ABOVE: *The center of my home. My simple white painted table serves as a place for snacks, feasts, business meetings, and art projects. The view of my garden is a constant source of inspiration and calming energy. The simple but glamorous crystal chandelier is both modern and classic. I found these folding chairs at the flea market and added comfy cushions. A glimpse of my sectional sofa shows how this room works as an all-in-one living space.*

PREVIOUS PAGE: *A moment of a little bit of everything. A classic painted upright piano does double duty as a cultural dumping ground. On top of the piano: a sculpture my mum made, inspired by Henry Moore; ballet slippers once used by my daughter; and abundant roses from my garden. Prom dresses and various theatrical hats and flowers are a constant in my house—I consider these installations as art. The turquoise Afghan throw works its way through my home.*

*As fancy as this may seem, for me it's a pretty typical place
setting for snack or feast. I like to take a moment to honor my
food by serving it on pretty plates. An abundance of flowers on
my table is a common sight, as are my special vintage linens.
While roses and peonies are my signature flowers, I have come
to appreciate the sturdiness, affordability and availability of
carnations. They are often my "go to" when an abundance of
flowers are needed, especially off-season.*

The signature foundation to my world of Shabby Chic will always be white and a chandelier, as evident in my living room where they are the anchors of my aesthetic: whiteness provides peace and a quiet base to layer upon; chandeliers bring beauty and I like the quirky juxtaposition of grandeur and elegance in humble surroundings. In the past, side chairs would have been flaky-painted old rocking chairs, but for now I am enjoying the juxtaposition of the classic Danish teak and basket-weave chairs, orchids, and an elegant LED sphere light on a thin, curved stem. But I am sure one day wonky chairs and cabbage roses will return. Regardless, I always hold the quintessential values of Shabby: invitingness, comfort, and evidence that the room is well lived in. For the moment though, a cleaner, curated flair takes center stage.

The dining room flows through from the living space and out into the garden, so it's a prime example of a combination room with a big, mushy sectional sofa in a nook; chairs found in a Texas flea market that are slightly more modern than my usual, albeit still with flaky wood; and a signature chandelier.

For many years I've slept in simplified Marie Antoinette–style bedrooms, but in my bedroom too, for now, I am breaking away from that tradition. The Rachel Ashwell Shabby Chic Couture Soho bed sits directly on the floor and has a modern, loft-type feel, but with the uniformity of the palette, breezy linens, and mushy white comfort, the bed would work on any stage from stately home to a raw loft. While the preconceived thought of modern is clean, lovely lines, in Shabby Modern it also has comfort and sensuality, which is evident thoughout my home.

In my garden, roses and lavender fight for supremacy and the result is a controled explosion of gorgeousness. Even though not much of a swimmer, I so enjoy the turquoise body of water as the center of my garden, surrounded by an abundance of roses and lavender. I like outhouses and meandering paths that lead to places where people can find sacred special spaces. This is a well-used house, thoughtfully created. If I'm on my own here or with a houseful, it's a home that is lovingly appreciated, a home that suits me and my life and for which I am daily grateful.

FROM LEFT TO RIGHT: *My mum would always send me a piece of vintage linen for every birthday and Christmas. I have quite a lovely collection that I cherish and use often. I do get great pleasure from collecting certain religious figures, but I'm selective about the facial expressions and look only for calm and contentment. This is a particular favorite of mine, and the fact she is painted white is a bonus. The quintessential Shabby Chic snow white linen chair. The perfect example of beauty, comfort, and function.*

White will always be a staple in my home but I do enjoy layering in pops of color by way of flowers, throws, and art. Recently I've enjoyed layering in more modern and structured chairs to complement the soft lines of upholstery. Art is an important part of the atmosphere in my home. The watercolor on the back wall, Two Lovers, by Kim McCarty, is one of my most beautiful, evocative pieces.

FROM LEFT TO RIGHT: *Blue silk lampshades sit beautifully on chandelier sleeves with fake but realistic wax drips; beauty is in the detail. The painting is by Kinley Winnaman; I love how she uses real silver leaf papers to give glamour to a pastel blue Buddha.*

ABOVE: *I recently painted a beige rug on my stairs; it's subtle and easily missed, but I so love it. I leave piles of whatever inspires me on the steps and around the house as my creative juices are always flowing. Books, tear sheets, fabrics, and flower petals are a common sight.*

RIGHT: *While white sheets or pretty flowers are my signatures, there is a boho island girl in me. This pewter stipple print speaks to that side of me.*

ABOVE: *My bedroom is forever changing, but it's always in the spectrum of white or soft pastels. A slipcovered Soho bed from the Shabby Chic collection sits directly on the floor, its modern lines complementing the soft and fluffy white bedding.*

RIGHT: *A glass lamp painted in white has modern flair and a traditional shape. The roses are clearly near the end of life but still shed beauty.*

A glimpse of my backyard. The simple blues of the pool, umbrella, and slipcovers on my chaises sit calmly with lavender and roses.

ECLECTIC ELEGANCE
PORTFOLIO

Over the past couple of decades, my own take on Shabby Chic has evolved and changed and the hodgepodgeness of it all is partly to do with the place I'm at in my own life. The house I live in now was not the house my children grew up in, but it's still our family home for precious gatherings and a resting place for lots of treasures.

In my search for clarity and simplicity, I'm bringing some modern twists into my home and some cleaner lines to the furnishings, while still embracing the tradition of the architectural bones inherited with my home. My truly breathtaking Shabby Chic garden is an orderly chaos of foliage and flowers that has a timeless beauty.

My eclectic home demonstrates how a little bit of all the elements: a touch of bohemian, a twist of modern, a traditional frou-frou and some ethnic eclecticism can all cohabit in my space—one that exhibits all the evolving diversities of Shabby Chic.

ABOVE: *This precious Holy Holy Holy mantel comes out once a year for a white Christmas in my home.*

PREVIOUS PAGE: *Intense sunlight spilling from a white room is almost heavenly. Light and snatched decorative moments are vital unsung heroes in the journey through a home.*

Candy-colored washed rugs are often found in my home.
Sometimes I love my bleached wooden floors free of anything,
but these are my go-to rugs when I am in the mood.
They are classic Turkish rugs, usually found in more
somber colors, but these have been put through a dye
process making for a whimsical palette.

Beautiful pieces come and go from my home for photo
shoots for my store. Some things are hard for me to part with,
and this sweet, button-backed Mable sofa was one of those.
So easy to find a spot for it, and make a magical moment.

*This unusual and beautiful Italian bed and nightstand
were only in my home fleetingly for a make-believe photo.
I love the proportions and pastel artwork. Modestly decadent.*

As I look back, Shabby Chic has been my life. I have raised it, alongside Jake and Lily, with the help of many along the way. Being a divorced mom with a business has been a lot of work, no doubt about it, and true lasting romances have been compromised by my romance with Shabby. But in the end it has suited me well. In hindsight I can look back on certain events and opportunities and know that if I had known then what I know now, I could have made better choices. But then I wouldn't have learned the lessons I did.

I have been inspired by strong, focused, hard-working people: artists, characters in novels, and my mum. I am proud of the status Shabby Chic has in the marketplace, but I hope those who like my brand enjoy it not as a status symbol, but for its soul and poetry. I plan to continue to evolve as an artist, businessperson, mother, and human. I have learned that my success comes from hard work, focus, and believing in the authentic truth of the story I tell. Whether the story is revealed through a sofa or through a flower, it all comes from my heart.

THANK YOU

To all who have come along the 25-year journey of The World of Shabby Chic.

I have been fortunate to have spent a life loving what I do. I may have led the way, but Shabby Chic is what it is because of all who have loved and supported me and appreciated the world of flaky paint, ruffles, mushy pillows and flowers.

Thank you to all who have been part of the Shabby Chic family and village. Whatever role you played, I thank you for choosing Shabby Chic for the chapters you were part of.

I thank vendors who have developed products for Shabby Chic, a mixture of scientists and artists.

I so appreciate the tireless community at flea markets around the world. I have enjoyed years of looking for treasures: mingling with dealers and pickers, swapping stories, and coming away with one-of-a-kind beauties which never fails to excite me, come rain or come shine.

To Jaimee Seabury for believing in me and in Shabby Chic, and for caring every day about every thing.

To my children, Jake and Lily, who have never known their worlds without Shabby Chic.

To my mum, for the fundamental lesson and acceptance of the beauty of imperfection. And for teaching me how to funnel my emotions into my art.

To Charles Miers, Ellen Nidy and the team at Rizzoli, along with Jill Cohen, Sarah Chiarot, and Alex Parsons, thank you for helping me bring the story of The World of Shabby Chic to life.

To Amy Neunsinger, thank you for the years of beautiful friendship and photos.

And a mention must go to a belt I bought twenty years ago, and have worn most every day since—my daily reminder that a choice of one is sometimes all that is needed.

PHOTOGRAPHY CREDITS

ALL PHOTOS BY *Amy Neunsinger (amyneunsinger.com)*
EXCEPT THE FOLLOWING:

COVER: *Carey More*

PERSONAL ARCHIVES,
p. 2, 9–11, 14, 18–19, 23–27, 32–35, 38, 47, 74, 85, 91, 105

ART STREIBER, ARTSTREIBER.COM
pp. 30–31, 52, 54, 77–79

ANNE MARIE ANNEMARIEPHOTOGRAPHY.COM
pp. 12, 72, 82–83

SARAH PANKOW
*title page, pp. 40, 60, 62–63, 65, 75, 86–88,
119, 224, 253, 268*

ANDREW MITCHELL
*pp. 17, 20, 56–57, 61, 66–68, 71, 89, 96, 101–102, 108, 111,
116–117, 121–122, 155, 202, 204, 207, 232–233, 237–238*

REED DAVIS, REEDDAVISPHOTOGRAPHY.COM
p. 100

LARS WANBERG
p. 126

RESOURCES

WWW.SHABBYCHIC.COM
WWW.THEPRAIRIEBYRACHELASHWELL.COM

RACHEL ASHWELL SHABBY CHIC COUTURE
1013 MONTANA AVENUE, SANTA MONICA, CA 90403
(310) 394-1975

RACHEL ASHWELL SHABBY CHIC COUTURE
83 WOOSTER STREET, NEW YORK, NY 10012
(212) 334-3500

RACHEL ASHWELL SHABBY CHIC COUTURE
3095 SACRAMENTO STREET, SAN FRANCISCO, CA 94115
(415) 929-2990

RACHEL ASHWELL SHABBY CHIC COUTURE
202 KENSINGTON PARK ROAD, LONDON W11 NR
011-20-7792-9022

RACHEL ASHWELL SHABBY CHIC COUTURE
2-22-16 SHINKO DAI 2 BLDG.
JINGUMAE
SHIBUYA-KU, TOKYO 150-0001
JAPAN
03-6447-4840

THE PRAIRIE B&B AND GIFT SHOP
5808 WAGNER ROAD
ROUND TOP, TX 78954
(979) 836-4975

WWW.LILYASHWELL.COM
FARROWANDBALL.COM
BENNISONFABRICS.COM

First published in the United States of America in 2015 by
Rizzoli International Publications, Inc.
300 Park Avenue South, New York, NY 10010
www.rizzoliusa.com

Text by Alexandra Parsons
Editor: Ellen Nidy
Designer: Sarah Chiarot
Design Coordinator: Kayleigh Jankowski

ISBN-13: 978-0-8478-4494-4
Library of Congress Control Number: 2014957718
2015 2016 2017 2018 2019 / 10 9 8 7 6 5 4 3 2 1

Printed and bound in China

Distributed to the U.S. trade by Random House